Pol

Policing the State

Democratic Reflections on Police Power Gone Awry,
in Memory of Kathryn Johnston (1914–2006)

Louis A. Ruprecht Jr.

CASCADE *Books* · Eugene, Oregon

POLICING THE STATE
Democratic Reflections on Police Power Gone Awry, in Memory of Kathryn Johnston
(1914-2006)

Cascade Books
An Imprint of Wipf and Stock Publishers
199 W. 8th Ave., Suite 3
Eugene, OR 97401

www.wipfandstock.com

ISBN 13: 978-71-62032-577-3

Cataloging-in-Publication data:

Ruprecht, Louis A.

Policing the state : democratic responses to police power gone awry, in memory of Kathryn Johnston (1914–2006) / Louis A. Ruprecht Jr.

xviii + 100p. ; 23cm.

ISBN 13: 978-71-62032-577-3

1. Police—United States. 2. Democracy—United States. 3. Police-community relations—United States. I. Title.

HV8139 .R87 2013

Manufactured in the U.S.A.

I have been studying how I may compare
This prison where I live unto the world.
And for because the world is populous
And here is not a creature but myself,
I cannot do it. Yet I'll hammer it out.
My brain I'll prove the female of my soul,
My soul the father, and these two beget
A generation of still-breeding thoughts,
And these same thoughts people this little world
In humors like the people of this world,
For no thought is contented. The better sort,
As thoughts of things divine, are intermix'd
With scruples, and do set the word itself
Against the word . . .

—WILLIAM SHAKESPEARE, *THE TRAGEDY OF KING RICHARD THE SECOND* V.5 (1597)

We who struggle with form and with America should remember Eidothea's advice to Menelaus when in the *Odyssey* he and his friends are seeking their way home. She tells him to seize her father, Proteus, and to hold him fast "however he may struggle and fight. He will turn into all sorts of shapes to try you," she says, "into all the creatures that live and move upon the earth, into water, into blazing fire; but you must hold him fast and press him all the harder. When he is himself, and questions you in the same shape that he was when you saw him in his bed, let the old man go; and then, sir, ask which god it is who is angry, and how you shall make your way homewards over the fish-giving sea."

For the novelist, Proteus stands both for America and the inheritance of illusion through which all men must fight to achieve reality; the offended god stands for our sins against those principles we all hold sacred. The way home we seek is that condition of man's being at home in the world, which is called love, and which we term democracy.

—RALPH WALDO ELLISON, "BRAVE WORDS FOR A STARTLING OCCASION" (1953)

As I would not be a *slave*, so I would not be a *master*. This expresses my idea of democracy. Whatever differs from this, to the extent of the difference, is no democracy.

—ABRAHAM LINCOLN, "ON SLAVERY AND DEMOCRACY" (c. 1859)

It is a commonplace in social criticism that modernity is typically experienced by ordinary people as a war between two great forces: the market and the state. We become resigned to being pawns moved about by economic forces and bureaucracies over which we have no control. The market and the state are the secular gods we fear and serve. We quarrel over which of them can save us from the other, and propitiate each in turn, but view ourselves for the most part as essentially powerless. The Katrina survivors in the Astrodome came close to having an extreme version of this experience. . . .

But this mythic picture does not capture the whole truth of what happened in the Astrodome, let alone the truth of our society. The morals of the Astrodome experience are rather different: no governmental bureaucracy, no capacity to constrain corporate power from dominating. No autonomous citizens' organization, no effective power for citizens. No effective power for citizens, no accountability for corporate, governmental, or nongovernmental power. No accountability, no way for power to be anything but arbitrary in its exercise and dehumanizing in its effects.

—JEFFREY STOUT, *BLESSED ARE THE ORGANIZED*, 76 (2010)

Contents

Dedication   ix

Acknowledgments   xiii

List of Primary Characters   xvii

1 Introduction   1

2 Jury Selection   18

3 The First Day   24

4 Policing by the Numbers, or, "Nine and Two"   28

5 The "War on Drugs"   36

6 New Technologies and the New Policing   44

7 "We're All in This Together"   48

8 Breaking the Case   64

9 The Human Cost   72

10 Defending the Indefensible   77

11 Deliberation and Judgment   82

Epilogue   89

Bibliography   101

Dedication

I WAS TWELVE YEARS old when I first read the transcript of a criminal trial. I was at a sleepaway summer camp in Maine, so I had the time for it. My father, who was then working primarily as a criminal defense attorney, was involved in a long and complicated trial that dragged on through much of the summer. A young ne'er-do-well who had recently joined a motorcycle gang was, so it appeared, being pinned with the murder of a rival gang member and his girlfriend, a murder that had actually been committed by higher-ups in the gang. He was eventually found innocent when the real criminals were driven to confessions of various sorts.

One way to tell that story would be to describe it as a success story for our judicial system. And so, in one important way, it was. My father, as a moral agent of the court, had something centrally to do with that.

But I see now that I read that transcript *not* from the perspective of my father, but rather from the perspective of *the jurors*. The transcript read at times like a murder mystery—it *was* a murder mystery, after all—and I was mesmerized by the enormity of the task of figuring out what I thought had happened, whom or what I believed, and who was to blame in my judgment. The details of the evidence at the murder scene were gruesome, highlighting the air of importance and the moral stakes of the case.

That said, it was the complexity of the human heart—caught forever between truths, half-truths, and outright falsehoods—that captivated me. I was reading an exercise in ethics and moral psychology, not just criminal law. That point stayed with me. It still does.

The social arenas in which lawyers and police lead their complicated lives are primarily dedicated to the virtue of justice. Good lawyers and good police embody that virtue in a very particular way, recognizing that the health of our political body depends on clarity about this matter, and its intimate relation to many other virtues.

My father, Louis Ruprecht, his wife, Judy Wahrenberger, and my brother, Cliff, are three such attorneys, each of whom recognizes the importance of justice to our fundamental social arrangements, as well as the law's sacred purpose in safeguarding the possibility that our most precious and fundamental social arrangements will be relatively just ones. My brother has become very interested in the new moral conundrums and the threats to privacy posed by electronic media; he works increasingly in the complicated realm of legal ethics. My stepmother possesses an acute eye for gender inequities in the workplace and for the legal remedies we have developed to address them. Four years ago, my father undertook to represent, on a volunteer basis, a detainee at the Guantanamo Bay facility, a quasi-client with whom he was unable to meet for more than a year. That client, a Libyan citizen who had fled Gaddafi's regime years earlier, was mistakenly identified as an enemy combatant; while proceedings were underway to secure a habeas corpus hearing, he was suddenly removed without prior notice and summarily returned to Libya, where he predictably disappeared into that regime's notorious gulag system.

After the revolution in Libya and Colonel Gaddafi's grisly death, my father tried unsuccessfully to learn of the man's whereabouts. As this book was going to press, Human Rights Watch managed to locate a cell phone number for this former detainee, but thus far it has proven eerily unresponsive. The most recent complicating factor came in the form of a widely circulated rumor in September 2012, suggesting that this man had taken a leadership role in the paramilitary group that was involved in the murderous attack on the U.S. embassy there. Shortly thereafter, the U.S. administration announced a shift in its understanding of the situation, confirming its belief that the attack was a terrorist attack masterminded by a local al-Qaeda cell, but exonerating the ex-Guantanamo detainee my father has still been unable to locate. While ultimately disavowed,[1] the rumor provides further evidence, if more were needed, of the dangers and the long-term damage that can be done by such willy-nilly ignoring of fundamental human rights. To be sure, one way to interpret this story is to conclude that this man was indeed an enemy combatant, from the outset; we simply did not know it until now. A more plausible interpretation is that we *made* him an enemy combatant; if his experience of U.S. justice were limited to the Guantanamo Bay facility, with its notorious record of enhanced interrogation and

---

1. The electronic thread may be followed at http://thecable.foreignpolicy.com/posts/2012/09/24/top_dem_no_evidence_former_gitmo_detainee_was_involved_in_benghazi_attack.

indefinite incarceration without formal charge, then it is easy enough to see how he might have been radicalized by this experience. So, as I will argue in this book, should we all be.[2] There is a relatively straight line that connects a society's most dehumanizing institutions and the violent chaos these generate in response; we make criminals in this way, not citizens. When we define away a class of person—as enemy combatant, as beyond rehabilitation, or as irredeemable—then we justify our own tendency to put such persons away forever with scarcely another thought. We also unwittingly create the very characters we fear the most: the secret and not-so-secret opponents of our institutions and the questionable values they too often embody. Justice, in short, is not a luxury; it is the fragile virtue designed to guard against such moral degradations, and the creation of vicious persons in their wake.

I have one more brother, Tom, who like me approaches such matters more from a literary than from a legal angle. He is a very gifted comedian; I am a less gifted (though aspiring) tragedian. So we tend to meet in the middle. Capturing the ambivalent tone of that middle is one of the tasks I've set myself in this book, as I try to explain at the end. Tom's capacity for inspiring laughter is what helps us all get by when confronted with stories like these.

This book is more punch in the gut than punch line; it represents my attempt to tell a story that helps make sense of the shocking metamorphosis taking place in the United States, whereby a constitutional republic grounded in radical democratic commitments has tended in the direction of a police state committed to keeping its own policing beyond the scrutiny of those institutions and those citizens we normally use to hold such power accountable. It is not a question of good guys and bad guys anymore, if it ever was. Rather, it is a piece of the massive industry of deregulation in which our nation has been engaged for the past thirty years, the emergence of an increasingly privatized "prison industrial complex" in these same years, and the massive new security apparatus with which we have been living since September 2001. We have constructed some very complicated new social arrangements that render all of us, in Simone Weil's elegant phrasing, "brothers and sisters in the same distress."[3]

2. The harrowing account of French torture techniques in the Algerian War was documented by Henri Alleg, one victim of wrongful detainment and weeks of systematic torture, in *The Question*, trans. John Calder, with an original preface by Jean-Paul Sartre and a new preface by James D. Le Sueur (Lincoln: University of Nebraska Press, 2006). That book, prohibited by French authorities only after more than twenty thousand copies had circulated, initiated an enormously important discussion of torture and military justice in France. I am indebted to my colleague Nadia Latif for this reference.

3. The phrase, *frères dans la même misère*, comes from her justly famous 1943 essay,

Just two days before Thanksgiving in 2006, a team of investigators from the Atlanta Police Department's Narcotics Unit served a "no-knock" search warrant at 933 Neal Street. It was already dark, just after 6:00 p.m., and they had some difficulty cutting through the burglar bars on the front door. When they entered the house, they saw a large figure to one side, half-hidden in shadows, who fired a single shot from a revolver into the ceiling over their heads. In the ensuing melee, thirty-nine shots were fired by the police involved in the raid; ricochets struck three of those same officers. Ms. Kathryn Johnston, the ninety-two-year-old owner of the home, was shot five or six times and died shortly thereafter. Eventually, an FBI investigation determined that the original application for the search warrant was bogus; to justify the warrant, police described a series of events that never took place, primarily the arrangement of a "controlled buy" at the address to confirm the presence of narcotics and the like. In the ensuing cover-up, the three police officers most directly involved in the case planted drugs at the scene, then tried to draw one of their paid informants into the larger circle of lies. Two of those officers eventually pled guilty to a variety of charges, including manslaughter.

The third, Arthur Tesler, claimed that he had no knowledge of the falsifications in the original application for the search warrant, and that he was drawn into the cover-up after the fact, primarily because his colleague had named him in the original warrant application without his knowledge. He had also learned not to make waves. Early in his career at the Atlanta Police Department, he had reported the racist and aggressive behavior of a fellow officer to his superiors, and in his opinion, was punished for this by being reassigned to the Atlanta international airport for fourteen months. I served as a juror at his trial, and this book constitutes my moral reflections, crafted as a sort of democratic citizen's reminiscence about that difficult experience and some of the more disturbing lessons—as well as some of the inspiration—I took away from it.

Mindful of where I come from, and on the eve of his seventy-fifth birthday, this book is dedicated to my father.

LAR
Atlanta, Georgia
October 2012

"The *Iliad*, or the Poem of Force," in *La Source Greque* (Paris: Gallimard, 1953) 26. In full the passage reads as follows: "Thus violence erases everyone it touches. It ends up seeming as external to those who wield it as it is to those who suffer it. And so was born the idea of a destiny before which executioners and their victims are similar in their innocence, victors and vanquished, brothers in the same distress."

Acknowledgments

I ENJOYED THE RARE privilege of offering a graduate seminar on the complex relationship between democracy, secularism, and religion in the spring of 2012, and this experience provided the final impetus for bringing this story into print. I am grateful to the participants in that seminar for sharpening my insights, and my moral sensibilities, in ways that I hope have found their way onto the page. I am thus obliged, and delighted, to record a debt of thanks to Leslie Andrews, Grene Baranco, Carrie Black, Brandon Bledsoe, Todd Hudson, Kyle Ingram, Sean Keane, Frank Miele, Josh Morrison, Nick Newell, Blake Singleton, Angela Stogsdill, and Omer Tasgeterin, for their inspired and inspiring presence there. Jason Baumunk, an undergraduate member of that seminar who was writing a marvelously creative Honors Thesis titled "Civic Poetics" in that same semester, provided me with a supremely thoughtful and instructive first reading of the manuscript. My graduate research assistant, Bishal Karna, prepared a wonderfully helpful survey of the major media reportage of the case between 2006 and 2008.

Sarah Levine has been a student, a research assistant, and a friend to me for many years; in addition to her close involvement with the weekly running of that seminar, she provided me with the great gift of her sensitivity and intelligence, both in conversation and in print. She read an earlier draft of this manuscript and offered countless insights that led to its improvement.

Universities are wonderful places in which to engage in such work, providing, as they do, the time and the collegiality necessary for it, and remaining committed, in their finer moments, to the sacred principles of democratic self-governance. Such commitments take time, lots of time. I am thus all the more in the debt of my closest colleagues for providing me with their time, with the intellectual atmosphere in which thoughts can marinate and mature, and in which difficult stories can be shared without rancor or withholding. Of particular value to me in this regard has been the democratic fellowship of my departmental colleagues: Wesley Barker, Abbas Barzegar, Molly Bassett, David Bell, Kate Daley-Bailey, Jon Herman, Claire Kooy, Nadia Latif, Ellen Logan, Kathryn McClymond, Monique Moultrie, Tim Renick, Felicia Thomas, and Isaac Weiner.

The unique commitment to scholarship and to a particular moral vision provided by the leadership of Georgia State University has also been invaluable. I am especially grateful to the Associate Dean of the College of Arts and Sciences, Carol Winkler, the Dean of that same College, William Long, and the University Provost, Risa Palm. I know that the humanities are having a rough time of it these days, in many academic and legislative settings; all three of those I have named here have been marvelous boosters of the humanities and the fine arts, and I am as indebted to them for the power of their personal examples as I am for their professional mentoring and support.

I am also grateful for the befriending I have received from any number of eloquent and impassioned friends of democracy. They lived out the virtues of that doubled friendship by going over previous drafts of this manuscript with their distinctive combination of sensitivity, care, and moral intelligence. A special word of thanks, then, for the readerly generosity, discerning judgment, and inspiring personal examples provided by Emily Dumler-Winckler, Molly Farneth, Lori Anne Ferrell, Jonathan Kahn, Katie Lofton, Shannon Mussett, Melanie Pavich, and Jim Winchester.

As will become very clear, I take the insights of Jeffrey Stout and Cornel West almost for granted as I think about many of the difficult matters I attempt to describe in this book, but I have tried to make my debts to both of them more explicit in the introduction and the epilogue. That both men have graced me with close friendship remains one of the most moving gifts that I owe to my academic life, and to Princeton University.

In the final stages of this manuscript's production, I was finally able to meet with the Reverend Anthony Motley, of the Lindsey Street Baptist Church here in Atlanta. He has been tireless in pursuing important institutional reforms in the name of protecting civil liberties in our city, and he has been especially eloquent in keeping the memory of Kathryn Johnston alive. It continues to be my hope, as I explain at several points in this book, that his call for an annual day of remembrance for what took place at 933 Neal Street on the 21st of November 2006, will be heeded so that the work of reconciliation to which he is committed may be better realized.

This is the second book that I have published with Wipf and Stock. Their editorial vision is a unique one, and I was especially pleased that they saw the connection that I see between the moral of this story and that vision. Their faith in, and commitment to, this project speaks to the remarkable range and subtlety of their religious and political sensibilities. My editor, Charlie Collier, was once my student at Emory University, long ago. His superb editorial eye and subtle intelligence have enabled us to switch roles in an effortless way that has been most inspiring to me. I am grateful to be his student now, and hope that the responsibility for editing this meandering manuscript has not been too taxing. For me his philosophical contributions, along with the brilliant editorial eye of Jacob Martin, proved invaluable.

My last word of thanks is the most important and heartfelt, despite its anonymity. I spent a terrible time in the presence of fourteen remarkable fellow citizens, men and women who, through their patient application of the skills of close attention and careful deliberation, helped restore my faith in our nation's still-unfolding experiment in pluralistic democracy, at a time when it was wavering. I am speaking of my fellow jurors in *State of Georgia v. Arthur Tesler.*

They know who they are.

Primary Characters

Judge Michael Johnson, Presiding Judge in Fulton County Superior Court (resigned)

Ms. Kellie Hill, Assistant District Attorney, Fulton County (now in Dekalb County)

Mr. Peter Odum, Assistant District Attorney, Fulton County (now in private practice)

Mr. William McKenney, Defense Attorney, McKenney & Froelich, Attorneys at Law

The Atlanta Narcotics Unit
(asterisks indicate that they testified in this trial)

Lieutenant BB*
Sergeant W. S.

Team One

C. B. (a male)
H. B. (a female)
———
Gregg Junnier (a white male)*
Jason (J. R.) Smith (a white male)
Arthur Tesler (a white male)*
———
G. S. (a black male)*

Primary Characters

M. G. (a black male)*
N. L. (a black male)

Fabian Sheats, narcotics dealer who first identified the 933 Neal Street address to Atlanta police

Alex White, Confidential Reliable Informant (CRI) who commonly worked with Officers Smith, Junnier, and Tesler

1

Introduction

We try to forget that capitalism itself makes more large decisions than any senator
with a program or a dream. We go down to the firehouse near the creek on those
Tuesdays in November. We sign in. One by one, we the imperfect have our say.

STEPHEN DUNN, "DEMOCRACY," IN *RIFFS & RECIPROCITIES* (1998)

THERE ARE MOMENTS IN the life of any modern moral community when
the word *democracy* has to become more than a mere word, if it is to
continue to mean anything at all. Now is such a time in the life of this
strange and wonderful North American experiment in representative,
pluralistic democracy. Ours was an experiment co-birthed with one of
the more expansive programs of institutionalized human enslavement the
world has ever seen; it was galvanized by an abolitionist movement and the
catastrophic destructiveness of the Civil War; and it was threatened anew
under the duress of Jim and Jane Crow. Clearly, democracy American-style
has developed with difficulty alongside of complex and interwoven debates
concerning the future of race and religion in America.

Despite this history, or perhaps because of it, one is hard-pressed to
find *any* American citizen, these days, who is opposed to "democracy." Everyone seems to buy the idea communicated so eloquently by John Dewey,
to the effect that the answer to democracy's ills is more democracy. But if
asked *why* we are so deeply committed to democracy as a political form, and
if we are asked *why* we are committed to its successful diffusion into other
parts of the world, even if this requires some very undemocratic-seeming

military intervention, then we grow strangely silent. In the fissures and fractures created by such silences, dangerous forces can fester.

This has always been the case. The ancient Athenians, who prided themselves on the great achievement of a very radical democracy (and not just radical by the standards of their day, but radical by our standards as well), were all too willing to use military force to impose constitutional reforms in other cities, islands, and occupied territories. For this reason, perhaps, their public philosophers were by no means unanimously enamored of the idea of democracy. Plato, the lyrical philosopher who did as much as anyone to make democracy a subject of theoretical reflection, seems high ambivalent about the idea. The democracy he knew had, after all, voted conscience in putting his dear friend Socrates to death. The representative agent for the democracy was a jury of his peers, free citizens all. This created a terrible dilemma that Plato devoted the remainder of his life to trying to resolve, though he never did.

On the one hand, Plato made the dialectic between freedom and enslavement central to his thought; Orlando Patterson has told this story with great eloquence, passion, and fluency.[1] Democracy was, for Plato, a fundamental political gesture in the direction of more complete and more robust freedom. The city was organized to create flourishing autonomous citizens who would need it less and less as they matured. Our fundamental purpose is to be free.

But large collections of free democratic citizens can make even larger and more violent mistakes. The absence of a professional governing class in Athens was a great achievement; it was also a grave and enduring problem. The Athenian assembly, especially under the pressure of the city's catastrophic war with Sparta (431–404 BCE), repeatedly voted to commit atrocities it later regretted. In one especially agonizing case—in the aftermath of a failed rebellion on the island of Lesbos—the assembly voted to massacre the entire adult male population of the island and to enslave the rest, making no distinction between those who had openly revolted and those who had supported Athenian interests, whether clandestinely or in the open. Ironically, the Athenians claimed this to be the result of truly democratic reasoning, since the alternative would have been to blame only the oligarchic ruling class of Mytilene. A trireme was dispatched to the

---

1. Orlando Patterson, *Freedom in the Making of Western Culture* (New York: Basic Books, 1991). This work builds upon his earlier volume *Slavery and Social Death: A Comparative Study* (Cambridge: Harvard University Press, 1982).

island with this somber ruling. "Next day, however," Thucydides informs us, "there was a sudden change of feeling and people began to think how cruel and how unprecedented such a decision was—to destroy not only the guilty, but the entire population of a state." The assembly met again and, with highly charged pathos appeals amply deployed by both sides, narrowly voted to reverse itself. A second trireme with word of this democratic reprieve was immediately fitted out and sent in all haste; making up most of the twenty-four-hour head start enjoyed by their less enthusiastic fellows, the Athenian warship arrived just as the original order had been read publicly and the first round of executions was being arranged. "So narrow had been the escape of Mytilene," Thucydides reports, with studied understatement.[2] A democratic assembly can be fickle, and can often function like a mob. People can be swayed by the persuasive power of eloquent speeches; truth can be enslaved or subject to the desire to convince.

The weak argument can be made stronger with effective rhetoric. Plato called these superficially strong speakers "sophists"; they often served in courts of law as what we might think of as lawyers today. Plato contrasted them with another class of wisdom-seekers he called "philosophers." In many cases, we contemporaries delight in condemning the alleged "sophistry" of lawyers, right up to the moment when we need their help; then we want the best sophist, or rhetorician, or lawyer that we can find. In Plato's day, it was rarely easy to say who stood on which side of the alleged divide separating sophists from philosophers. According to the report Plato provides in his *Apology*, Socrates presented himself as a philosopher, a

2. This terrifying tale is reported by Thucydides in his classic text, *The Peloponnesian War*, bk. III. 36–49, a text that Thomas Hobbes famously translated well before he wrote his masterwork of (anti)democratic political philosophy, *Leviathan*. Commenting on the value of the work he translated, Hobbes notes rather coyly, "in history, actions of *honour* and *dishonour* do appear plainly and distinctly, which are which; but in the present age they are so disguised that few there be, and those very careful, that be not grossly mistaken about them" (4).

For discussion of the Mytilenian affair, see *Hobbes's Thucydides*, ed. Richard Schlatter (New Brunswick: Rutgers University Press, 1975) 194–204, and *The Peloponnesian War*, trans. Rex Warner (New York: Penguin, 1954) 212–23. It is noteworthy that a brief discussion of the limited deterrent value of the death penalty was one centerpiece of the new Athenian position as reported by Thucydides: as with individual criminals, so too with renegade cities; that was the new comparative idea, one also taken up by Plato in the *Republic*, bk. 2.

A good discussion of the models of democratic deliberation depicted in this scene is Clifford Orwin, *The Humanity of Thucydides* (Princeton: Princeton University Press, 1994) 142–62.

truth-teller committed to the moral health of his city, who offered it the difficult therapy of critical interrogation, the challenging back-and-forth of rational enquiry. But the jury of his peers that was to vote first on his guilt or innocence, and then secondly on what his punishment should be, took a different view. They mistrusted his artfulness with words, believing (by a narrow margin, to be sure) that he was himself a rhetorician and a sophist, and they condemned him as such.

Both names, *sophist* and *philosopher*, are built upon the noble Greek word for wisdom, *sophia*. But we would do well to note how that simple word can be made to mean radically different things. What is a wise man? What is a wise guy? The first phrase sounds like a compliment, the second like a complaint. Philosophers thought that sophists were wise guys pretending to be wise men. Sophists thought the same thing about the philosophers. It was often impossible for democratic Athenians listening to the two sides debating the question to decide which was which. Words can be made to dazzle and confuse. Discerning judgment thus became one of the most important virtues for the democratic citizen to cultivate in public encounters of all kinds.

The reasons for this had everything to do with that marvelous, and very nearly instinctive, Athenian suspicion of a professional political or military class. When I referred to the Athenian democracy as "radical," that is primarily what I had in mind. Fully half of the political positions in Athens were chosen by lot. The implications of that simple fact are astonishing. It meant that every free citizen of Athens was deemed *capable* of doing the political tasks necessary to maintaining the health and wealth of the city. And it meant that every free citizen would be *expected* to take their turn. One of the most constant of those forms of political involvement was jury duty. The Athenians, very much like modern Americans, were notoriously litigious people who took one another to court all the time. Juries could be quite large, and they met almost daily. The assembly met every ten days or so. Each year a sort of senate of five hundred citizens was appointed to organize the daily governance of the city, and fifty of them at a time lived together in the center of town in order to deal with any emergencies that came up, day or night. In short, the Athenians were expected to be active democratic citizens, virtually all the time.

When it worked, it worked brilliantly. When it failed, it failed spectacularly. When a jury of perhaps five hundred citizens found Socrates guilty of violating the religious and moral norms of the city, the Athenian democracy announced a rather confusing conception of the state's relationship to religion. Socrates was accused of introducing new gods into the city; the city of Athens regularly did the same. Socrates was accused of disrespecting the traditional gods of the city; most Athenians took a dim view of that. After finding Socrates guilty, when those same jurors had to vote on a penalty, and when Socrates seemed to provoke them further by suggesting a reward rather than a punishment, they voted to have him executed. And he was. Democracy can work hand in glove with entrenched religious interests, and it can exercise its policing function with the same brutal force we associate with empires or tyrannies. Athens was both an empire and a democracy, strangely enough, at this time. Socrates' execution thus was remembered later on as an essential turning point in the life of a short-lived experiment in radical democracy. When the Athenian empire collapsed so spectacularly, the philosophers and sophists managed to think their way into a new and very different way of understanding the importance and imagining the future of the city they so admired.

In short, they turned Athens into a university town. For many centuries subsequent to Socrates' execution in 399 BCE, students from around the Mediterranean basin—as well as farther inland, and farther to the east—would make a pilgrimage of sorts to the very city that had killed the founder of ancient philosophy. They would pay to study with the heirs to this Socratic way of life, wise guys and wise men alike, and they would do so in what remained, nominally at least, a democratic city. The marvelous modes of thinking this remarkable city made possible—a place for reflection, study, and self-creation—flourished for centuries. Central to the work in which these wisdom-seekers of various stripes engaged were questions of the relationship between virtue and philosophy, religion, and democratic politics. The goal was a virtuous life lived in each of these important and overlapping social arenas.

Now clearly, much has changed since Socrates engaged his fellow citizens in the difficult work of question-posing and values clarification, since Plato reflected on the moral and democratic meaning of his dear friend's execution by the city, and since Aristotle attempted to provide an encyclopedic coherence to the various things that *his* teacher, Plato, had taught him. After Aristotle, and the radical differentiation among the various philosophical schools (especially the Cynics, the Skeptics, and the Stoics), Athens remained for centuries the place to go, if you could afford it, to get a liberal arts education. In our finer moments, America remains that singular destination and intellectual pilgrimage site for many of the world's finest (and wealthiest) students today.

Nonetheless, in between Socrates' execution and our own times looms a second execution—orchestrated this time by the Roman imperial state apparatus rather than the Athenian democracy. I am thinking, of course, of Jesus' crucifixion in Jerusalem in roughly 30 CE. Out of this second traumatic experience of what was recognized in retrospect as a tragic political mistake, a new and very different religion emerged: Christianity. That religion was destined to change a great deal in the ancient world, a world created by this curious commingling of Greek philosophy, Roman empire, and Roman law. Viewed one way, the rise of Christianity in the fourth century changed everything in the ancient Roman world. And yet, viewed another way, it changed very little. Roman citizens continued to eat the same way, to dress the same way, to marry the same way, and even to deliberate about ethics and politics in the same way.[3] The striking dialectic of slavery and freedom that Plato had initiated continued to be a major preoccupation of traditional Romans and the newer Christian kind of Roman alike. Freedom continued to be seen as the primary point of politics, in Rome as it had been in Athens.

That is why the older story of modern secularization and revolutionary modern politics didn't have the situation quite right. It was not the case that the early modern period—for all of the radicalism of the revolutions that broke out in England in 1688, in North America in 1776, and in France in 1789—was a radical break with the past, especially the religious past. Just the opposite, in a way. The astonishing world in which a pope could be called "anti-Christ" in print, or a king could be executed by the people under the aegis of the rule of law, was actually framed in terms that Christians shared, by and large, with their pagan predecessors. What appears to have happened in the early modern period is that a religious discourse of slavery and freedom was translated into more secular terms. The most important of these translations involved the language of "rights." And in the name of such determined *individual* human rights, we have witnessed the two seismic social revolutions that have so dramatically altered social life

---

3. No one has done more to underline the astonishing continuities between the pre-Christian and Christian world of the western Roman empire than Peter Brown. In his latest work, *Through the Eye of a Needle: Wealth, the Fall of Rome, and the Making of Christianity in the West, 350–550 AD* (Princeton: Princeton University Press, 2012), Brown argues that things did not change significantly until the sixth and seventh centuries when, for the first time, we can begin to speak of the emergence of a distinctively Christian culture, well after the cultural translations I have in mind were complete.

in the modern world: the abolition of institutions of human enslavement in the nineteenth century, and the advent of feminism and the full political inclusion of women in the twentieth century.

The power of this language of rights, and its philosophical subtlety, is easy to miss. It is well captured by the complex character of the U.S. Constitution. It is important to recognize that our Constitution is composed of two separate documents that are designed to work at cross-purposes. The Constitution describes the political arrangements, and a complicated balance of powers, whereby most (though admittedly not all) of our political decisions are rendered by majority vote. This is the democratic heart of the U.S. Constitution, and this is why the structure of the legislative branch is described first in it. The Senate and House of Representatives are the peoples' houses. But over against this enormously significant democratic constitutional arrangement stands the Bill of Rights.

The important new word there is *rights*. Rights name those individual prerogatives that no one may take away—not a king, not a queen, not a pope, not a priest, and most important of all, not even a democratic majority that has voted someone's rights away. The Constitution works toward majority rule and social consensus. The Bill of Rights protects individuals from the excesses of those same majorities. The system is designed to protect the future Socrateses and Mytilenes of the world from the fickleness and the mistaken judgments an ancient democracy made, or nearly made, two and a half millennia ago.

～

I noted at the outset that there are moments in the life of any modern moral community when the word *democracy* has to become more than a mere word, if it is to continue to mean anything at all. In my own experience, 2004 represented a particular watershed in my thinking about the democracy in which I live. Two books were published in that year that were destined to change the way I think about such matters forever. The first of them was Jeffrey Stout's *Democracy and Tradition*,[4] a bracing account of the distinctive virtues and practices that are supposed to go together with, and be promoted by, democratic citizenship. The second was Cornel

---

4. Jeffrey Stout, *Democracy and Tradition* (Princeton: Princeton University Press, 2004). Stout has recently extended this analysis of moral language with a study of power arrangements and grassroots organizing titled *Blessed Are the Organized* (Princeton: Princeton University Press, 2010).

West's *Democracy Matters*,[5] which offers a deep and prophetic criticism of the current arrangements that constitute an American form of imperialism, and the economic inequities upon which such a system is most commonly built. Both men think a great deal about democracy, worry a great deal about ethno-racial justice, and identify what they take to be the utterly corrosive role that contemporary forms of rapacious capitalism are playing in our increasingly plutocratic politics.

Stout's message was very simple, but all the more eloquent for its simplicity. There are *habits* that are supposed to come with democratic citizenship. And there are *questions* that we are expected to pose habitually, as well. These habits provide profound moral content, what Hegel referred to as "ethical substance"; they have everything to do with the sorts of people we aspire to be, individually and in relation to one another. Justice, as Reinhold Niebuhr[6] pithily observed, is what love demands in the presence of more than one neighbor.[7] In other words, the secularized translation of Christian

5. Cornel West, *Democracy Matters: Winning the Fight against Imperialism* (New York: Penguin, 2004).

6. Reinhold Niebuhr was a Christian ethicist whose political theory has come in for renewed attention and interest since he has been understood, for better or worse, as a significant influence on President Barack Obama's evolving political attitudes. Niebuhr's so-called Christian Realism is nicely discussed in relation to the current geopolitical and fiscal crises in a special volume of *Soundings: An Interdisciplinary Journal* 95.4 (2012). It is instructive that Cornel West recently returned to take up a position at Union Theological Seminary, where Niebuhr served for many years as professor of applied Christianity.

7. Niebuhr began working out this idea in 1935, in his *An Interpretation of Christian Ethics* (New York: Seabury, 1935, 1963) 62–122, where he referred to the ideal of Christian love (*agape*) as an "impossible ethical ideal" that nonetheless informed reasoned commitments to justice and equality in various social settings, political and economic alike. What he calls the pragmatic and perfectionist perspectives "both have their own legitimacy," he admitted, "[b]ut moral confusion results from efforts to compound them" (ibid., 114). Niebuhr would later refine this view by concluding that love and justice were "dialectically" related, such that justice is always judged in relation to the perfectionist demands of Christian love, or *agape*; this is a major theme of his Gifford Lectures, published as *The Nature and Destiny of Man*, 2 vols. (New York: Scribner, 1941–43), especially in a chapter titled "The Kingdom of God and the Struggle for Justice," 2:244–86. In later occasional writings, Niebuhr would suggest that justice demanded "tragic" choices in a way that love did not, and still more importantly for my purposes, that "the 'sense of justice' is an expression of the law of love *within the limits of law*" (italics mine).

This last comment, published in 1950, is quoted by Paul Ramsey in his critical engagement with Niebuhr's conception of law, both natural and supernatural, in *Nine Modern Moralists* (Englewood Cliffs, NJ: Prentice Hall, 1962) 111–47, at 125. The relation between law and love was further elucidated by Ramsey in *Basic Christian Ethics* (Chicago: University of Chicago Press, 1950) 35–45, 157–66, 343–51.

love is "justice," although it must be admitted that no perfectly satisfying "translation" of such a kind is possible. The idea is that democratic citizens are called to express lovingkindness in a compassionate ethic of mutuality, combining social care with moral responsibility.[8]

When Jesus was reputedly asked what the single greatest Jewish commandment was, he appeared to answer with two, not one: loving God; and loving one's neighbor as oneself.[9] The idea appears to be that our moral attention needs to be directed vertically and horizontally at the same time. Stout secularizes this same insight, by insisting that modern democratic citizens should be animated by two similarly fundamental ethical concerns. First, from the standpoint of verticality, we must work to avoid even the appearance of anything that constitutes dominating relationships. The great "other" to the free democratic citizen is for this reason symbolized by the enslaved person. Enslavement is the very paradigm of a dominating relationship; Plato understood that very well.[10] What makes domination relatively easy to recognize is the absence of any accountability structures, creating the possibility of exercises of power in ways that are literally beyond accounting. And that brings us to the horizontal dimension, involving a democratic habit modern Americans must learn to cultivate anew. When we seek to determine where power (whether monetary, political, military, or police) tends to be concentrating, then our instinctive reaction to that situation should be the nearly automatic follow up: how we are going to hold accountable such power that is concentrating in such a way just *there*? Viewed this way, democratic life begins to appear as a never-ending ethical world of call-and-response.

Stout and West share the concern that "plutocracy" names what most ails the current version of North American democracy. Monetary power

8. During the singular stresses of the Second World War, Reinhold Niebuhr pressed the point this way: "But modern democracy requires a more realistic philosophical and religious basis, not only in order to anticipate and understand the perils to which it is exposed; but also to give it a more persuasive justification. *Man's capacity for justice makes democracy possible; man's capacity for injustice makes democracy necessary*. . . . [My views are] informed by the belief that a Christian view of human nature is more adequate for the development of a democratic society than either the optimism with which democracy has become historically associated or the moral cynicism which inclines human communities to tyrannical political strategies." *The Children of Light and the Children of Darkness* (New York: Scribner, 1944) xi, xiii; italics mine.

9. See the exchanges described in Mark 12:28–34; Matthew 22:34–40; Luke 10:25–28.

10. See the witty and provocative essay by Norman Austin, "Hellenismos," *Arion, Third Series* 20.1 (2012) 5–36.

has been concentrating for the past thirty years in ways that render a new class, the billionaire (a term, and a concept, that did not exist fifty years ago), literally beyond the reach of law or order. Such persons, possessing wealth well in excess of the budgets of smaller nation-states, can affect global politics and can do so in ways that are rendered invisible, and therefore beyond accounting. Stout put it this way, back in 2004:

> Meanwhile, multinational corporations have become the latter-day equivalents of the East India Company. We now have government for the corporations, by the corporations, but almost no government *of* the corporations. That's what "deregulation" means. "Corporate despotism" may be the best name for the mode of government we now have, but the term "democracy" remains a good name for a people's disposition to hold one another, their leaders, and their corporations responsible for their acts. It may be a latent disposition, but it's still worth singling out and cultivating to the degree we can.[11]

In other words, the multinational corporation is hard to regulate precisely because it is multinational. Nearly all of our regulatory institutions are housed within nation-states. Parked safely offshore, money (and the power it provides) floats free of ethical or political constraint. The absolute power of kings and queens has been replaced by the absolute power of a new financial class. The Wall Street fiasco, the serial collapse of an allegedly professional and well-regulated banking system in Iceland, Ireland, Greece, Italy, Spain, and the United States, as well as the Occupy Movement, and debates over tax reform are all of a piece.[12]

To put it a bit crudely, money is in danger of mattering more than democracy. Add security to the mix—and in English we have blurred the meaning of *security* with the related term *securities*—and you have the recipe for a potential social disaster.

11. The comment was made at the first large panel discussion of *Democracy and Tradition* in November 2003. See a transcript of that discussion (with Stanley Hauerwas, Richard Rorty, and Cornel West) in *The Journal of the American Academy of Religion* 78.2 (2010) 433.

12. Michael Lewis has been a remarkably thoughtful, as well as provocative and funny, observer of this complex terrain. See his analysis of the Wall Street crash in *The Big Short: Inside the Doomsday Machine* (New York: Norton, 2010), as well as his analysis of the global credit and banking crisis in *Boomerang: Travels in the New Third World* (New York: Norton, 2011).

For a more substantive (by which I mean simply less narrative and prosaic) analysis of what has been happening over the past thirty years, see David Harvey, *A Brief History of Neoliberalism* (New York: Oxford University Press, 2005).

How these realities affect the average citizen—the so-called 99 per-cent—is difficult to gauge at times.[13] Hardly an economist myself, I have what I hope is a slightly simpler take on the nature of the current situation. It is a situation that would have been very clear in Athens under the city's radical democracy, since central to their democratic reforms was a redis-tribution of wealth and an emphatic expansion of all citizens' participation in good governance.[14] The ancient philosophers were of one mind in their conviction that once the wealthiest citizens possessed more, many times over, than what the poorest possessed, then dangerous social stratification, and the natural grievances this creates, would almost inevitably result.[15]

In our world, the differential between the richest and poorest among us is a factor of millions, not fives or tens. That is what makes the old story told by Milton Friedman and other neoliberal economists seem so topsy-turvy.[16] In this economist's story of freedom, early modern *capitalism* was

13. I note with appreciation the eighty-seven-page report by Carmen DeNavas-Walt, Bernadette D. Proctor, and Jessica C. Smith, "Income, Poverty, and Health Insurance Coverage in the United States: 2010," issued by the U.S. Department of Commerce in September 2011 and based on information from the 2010 U.S. Census. See http://www.census.gov/prod/2011pubs/p60–239.pdf.

14. This began under the legendary legal reforms of Solon, described by Diogenes Laertius in his *Lives of the Eminent Philosophers*, trans. R. D. Hicks, 2 vols., Loeb Classical Library (Cambridge: Harvard University Press, 1972) 46–69.

But the culmination of these early economic reforms were the massive structural re-forms enacted by Cleisthenes. See Pierre Lévêque and Pierre Vidal-Naquet, *Cleisthenes the Athenian: An Essay on the Representation of Space and Time in Greek Political Thought from the End of the Sixth Century BCE to the Death of Plato*, with further essays by Corne-lius Castoriadis, trans. David Ames Curtis (Atlantic Highlands, NJ: Humanities, 1996).

15. This is very clearly enunciated both in Plato's account of the democracy's emer-gence from a prior oligarchic regime in *Republic* 330b–331b, 555b–558c, and in Aristo-tle's *Politics* 1256a1–1259a36, a discussion of property (and acquisition more generally) that concludes with the essential distinction between the love of wisdom (as well as virtue) and the love of money.

16. See Milton Friedman with Rose D. Friedman, *Capitalism and Freedom*, 2nd ed. (Chicago: University of Chicago Press, 1982). Friedman's defense of what he takes to be classical liberal political theory (5–6, though we would call it "neo-liberal" today) asserts an intimate connection between economic and political liberty that hinges on two sacred principles: first, that "the scope of government must be limited" (2); and second, that "government power must be dispersed" (3). In the name of the deregulatory regime these principles entail, Friedman offers a lyrical defense of "competitive capitalism—the organization of the bulk of economic activity through private enterprise operating in a free market—as a system of economic freedom and a necessary condition of politi-cal freedom" (4). History plays an unusual role in this analysis. Though he admits that "historical evidence by itself can never be convincing" (11), Friedman invokes historical

the key to the emergence of modern rights language and modern democratic revolutions.[17] The idea is that capitalism depends on full transparency, and obedience to our contractual arrangements. Banks have names like "Fidelity" and "Trust" for a reason on this view. Adam Smith, who was a theorist both of modern capitalism *and* of modern ethics,[18] articulated a view of capitalism that defended it as a system organized to lift the lowest members of a society to heights previously undreamed of. Capitalism was the way to assist the greatest number of individuals, in his judgment. And sympathy was, he believed, the most universal of all moral sentiments.

That story is highly suspect these days, and not just among the Marxists. Some of Smith's analysis hinged on articles of faith, not arguments. And the system of global capitalism he described looked more benevolent in direct proportion to how much the role of imperialism and market colonialism among the European gunpowder empires was ignored.

---

precedent to establish some astonishing generalizations with some frequency.

"The great advances of civilization," he observes, *whether in architecture or in painting*, in science or literature, in industry or agriculture, have never come from centralized government" (3, italics mine). To say this is to think the Italian Renaissance only after thinking away the Medici in Florence or the enormous papal patronage state centered in Rome. Later, he suggests that "[h]istorical evidence speaks with a single voice on the relation between political freedom and the market. I know of no example in time or place of a society that has been marked by a large measure of political freedom, and that has not also used something comparable to a free market to organize the bulk of economic activity" (9). I have shown how precisely the opposite was the case in what Friedman too considers "the golden age of Greece" (10).

Friedman's conclusion is that we in the United States have evolved a political system in which "[t]he catchwords became welfare and equality rather than freedom" (5); the result is the denial of what he thinks self-evident: that "economic freedom is an end in itself" (8). It is that setup, carrying with it the implication that we cannot reasonably work for all three (freedom, welfare, and equality) at the same time, and that conclusion, regarding the end of economic freedom, that I wish to question here.

17. The challenge, of course, is to establish a *causal* connection between the emergence of modern capitalism and the rights revolutions, especially as it relates to the abolition of human enslavement. For a subtle and nuanced analysis of the way in which capitalism provided a "precondition" for abolitionist movements, one involving a significant shift in "perception" and "cognitive style," see Thomas L. Haskell, "Capitalism and the Origins of the Humanitarian Sensibility," *The American Historical Review* 90.2 (1985) 339–61 (Part 1) and 90.3 (1985) 547–66 (Part 2). I am indebted to my colleague, Nadia Latif, for this reference.

18. Smith wrote *The Theory of Moral Sentiments*, ed. D. D. Raphael and A. L. Macfie (Indianapolis: Liberty Classics, 1976) in 1759, well before his far more famous study of global capitalism, *An Enquiry into the Nature and Causes of the Wealth of Nations*, ed. Edwin Cannan (New York: Modern Library, 1937).

Closer to home and closer to our own day and age, we have seen that banks are every bit as capable of being unfaithful and untrustworthy as any other power broker. The temptation to be vicious, not virtuous, increases in direct proportion to the absence of accountability structures—what is more commonly referred to as "regulation." As Stout observes, unregulated wealth becomes unaccountable power. And the results for a democratic people have been harrowing.

My concern is that the power and influence of the financiers and the entire business sector extend well beyond what we can see. People are attracted to the United States to become rich; businesses are attracted to the United States to be free (of regulation). Increasingly, the paradigms we all use, most of the time, derive from business models and the business world. We have adopted quantitative modes of assessment and oversight even in social arenas where they cannot possibly work well. The three most important of these social arenas are education, medicine, and policing. The results of strictly crunching the numbers to measure success in these three areas have been terrible. Reduce a person to a number, then make the number part of an aggregate, then turn the aggregate into a trend, then use that manufactured trend to set social policy. A more *un*democratic mode of reasoning and regulating is scarcely imaginable.

This is the world where assessment regimes like "No Child Left Behind" work best when teachers "teach to the test," or when administrators agree to falsify test results in the aggregate by elevating the numbers to get the trends they want, in the sure knowledge that this lie will result in access to more money for the school. Our current debates over health care often reveal a similarly and exclusively quantitative mentality. We have the most expensive health care system in the world, not, as is often alleged, the best one. Medicine is a matter of care, first and foremost, not a matter of mathematics. Our inability to distinguish these matters—big numbers and big money from a virtuous system of human care—is one part of the moral epidemic of our time, the era of "strictly business" models of accountability and assessment, the age of the spread sheet.

⁓

In this book, I endeavor to tell this story in a manner defined by my own evolving democratic commitments, and in an unexpected (though intimately related) social arena: modern state policing. Just as I will work to avoid the simplistic "heroes and villains" account of modern lawyers, I will work at least as hard to avoid assessing the police in accordance to the standards of such a myth. We all need good lawyers when we need a lawyer. We all need good police when we need the police. What constitutes their goodness is the central question, as it has been since Plato put the question. Tragically, that fundamentally moral question has often been reduced to a question of quantitative assessment as well. The idea becomes this: good police arrest a lot of people and serve a lot of search warrants. And yet breaking into a private home is the most dangerous thing that most police officers will ever do—for them, and for our democracy. Our system of policing is thus now so skewed that it is designed actually to create more danger and, inevitably, to foster potential injustice. The police officers themselves are as much the victims of this system of assessment as the citizens whose rights are currently under siege—brothers and sisters in the same distress.

This book tells the story of how that regime resulted in one of the two Atlanta Narcotics Unit teams breaking into a private home and firing thirty-nine rounds in total at a ninety-two-year-old woman whose home was subject to an illegal search, under the cover of a so-called no-knock warrant. Ms. Kathryn Johnston was shot five or six times and died almost instantly in her home. Three police officers were also shot in a melee of their own making. The cover-up in which three of these Narcotics officers engaged was soon *un*covered by the FBI. Since there is rarely honor among thieves, the three men eventually turned to saving their own respective skins, if not their reputations or their careers. Two of the men confessed, one turned state's evidence, and they are currently serving terms of six and ten years' incarceration, respectively. A number of other officers confessed to their complicity later on, or were dismissed by the Atlanta Police Department. The third officer involved in the original cover-up, Arthur Tesler, was charged with three lesser offenses, declared himself to be innocent on all counts, and was tried before a jury of his peers in a four-week trial on which I served as one of fifteen jurors. He was found guilty of one of the three charges of which he had been indicted and sentenced to the maximum penalty of five years by the presiding judge. The judgment was later overturned by the Georgia Court of Appeals, though by then Officer Tesler had pled guilty to federal charges as well.

The tragic results of this one falsified search warrant should not distract us from the massive crisis in civil liberties that such no-knock warrants represent. The uninvited presence of armed representatives of the state in your private residence is specifically named in our Bill of Rights as a matter of the gravest concern (Amendment 3). So are "unreasonable searches and seizures" (Amendment 4). We have a system in which the state may indeed seize our property (through taxation, confiscation of money or property, and so on), may suspend our liberty (by placing us under arrest and/or imprisoning us), and may even take our lives (we are highly unusual among Western nations in still having a death penalty in most states). But the state may only engage in these enormous and consequential intrusions into our personal lives through "due process of law" (Amendment 5, a mandate that was extended to each of the individual states by Amendment 14). The judiciary branch of the government, embodied in our judges and in our courts, is charged with the all-important responsibility of overseeing such activities; the courts determine whether due process of law was followed prior to the state's police power interfering with so fundamental a liberty as being left alone in our home; a judge must issue a search warrant before the police can serve under its dangerous conditions. That is the regulatory system that broke down in Atlanta, with tragic consequences. As I will show, even modern technology (in the form of computers) played a surprising role in the catastrophic breakdown of accountability structures there.

I just so happened to be out of town when Ms. Johnston was killed in November 2006. Thus I missed all of the initial reportage of the case—and the extensive public outrage and street protests that the case understandably produced. Democratic citizens are supposed to know not just how to pose questions but also how to determine when it is time to march, and so to demand redress of our legitimate grievances; this right and responsibility is also named explicitly in our Bill of Rights (Amendment 1). As a member of the jury at trial, I was not permitted to read newspapers or watch television, so I did not know how the trial was being reported either. While I have consulted some of those materials now in the preparation of this book, the main sources for this book are the extensive notes I took each day—transcribed at lunchtime, and pondered each evening—while the trial was taking place. It seemed an important enough story to record for further reflection, offering evidence as it does of the fragile state of our (or any) democracy, and about the social and juridical arrangements we have developed in order to enable the necessary oversight of the policing function of a modern industrial state.

Now, I think, is a most fitting time for this story to be told. Jeffrey Stout and Cornel West had prepared me in 2004 for what I was to learn—and quite frankly, to wish I did not know, at times—about what transpired in Atlanta in 2006. It was 2008, at the trial, when I learned what I now know, and it has taken me four years of further reading and reflection to come to terms with that knowledge.

After further arrests and dismissals of police officers ordered by the new police chief, George Turner, Kathryn Johnston's family was awarded a $4.9 million payment by the City of Atlanta in August 2010. The family, represented by Ms. Johnston's niece, Sarah C. Dozier,[19] received an initial payment of $3 million, and were to be paid the remaining $1.9 million in the summer of 2012. I honestly do not know what to make of that sum, nor of the idea of financial reparation for such violent wrongs.[20] It seems of a piece with the very quantitative reasoning I worry about most, and in any case, the sudden arrival of such enormous sums can do strange things to families and friends. It also invites the perception, false in this instance, that the case is now closed. As I will suggest in conclusion, there is much that remains *un*done in addressing the catastrophic institutional failures that created the conditions that led to Ms. Johnston's death. Nonetheless, while the circle inscribing this tragic story will never be completely closed, the final payment to her family does represent a moment of tentative closure, for the city if not the family. So does the recent release of Mr. Tesler from prison, and his return to Atlanta. It seemed an appropriate time, then, for me to set down a proper record of what happened in November 2006, based on my understanding of the testimony of those who were most closely involved.

I have thought a great deal more about Athens, a city I greatly admire for its extraordinary experiment in combining the moral sentiments of a radical democracy with the tragic sensibilities of a citizenry schooled on ancient drama and the unique discursive wisdom of the philosophers— wise guys and wise men alike. I have also thought a great deal, and in a substantially different way, about my own country, a country I also admire for its remarkable experiment in radical, pluralistic democracy and the commingling of constitutional democratic principles with the singular protections of a Bill of Rights.

19. For the substance of Ms. Dozier's complaint against the city of Atlanta, see *Sarah C. Dozier v City of Atlanta* (December 21, 2009). Online: http://www.atlantaunfiltered. com/wp-content/uploads/2010/05/kathryn-johnston-undisputed-facts.pdf.

20. It is a source of singular astonishment that Ms. Johnston's pastor (and former congressional candidate), the Reverend Markel Hutchins, sued Ms. Johnston's family for $500,000 shortly after the cash award was announced and the first installment delivered (this was in late August 2011). His argument was that he served as the family's counselor and spokesperson throughout the tragedy with the clear understanding that he would receive 10 percent of any settlement they eventually received. Such a story links Christian churches and blood money in ways too intimate to be comforting.

Our contemporary moral sensitivities seem to me to stand in need of that marvelous leavening that the spirit of old Athens—its radical democratic commitments, its tragic sensibility, and its commitment to philosophical wisdom—can provide. The unique moral sentiments cultivated by a combined commitment to democratic, tragic, and philosophical wisdom are powerful and profound.[21] I learned this lesson anew while serving on a jury with my peers; I was taught this lesson anew *by* my peers. We are called to remember the spirit of old Athens in the videos that most every citizen of the United States is required to watch when first called to jury service. (We are not invited to recall what one of those juries did to Socrates; we probably should be). Jury duty remains the purest form of citizens' service as defined in terms set by the radical democracy in classical Athens. There is nothing quantitative about the assessment such juries provide; it is a very slow and deliberative process that hinges on what can seem like an excessive amount of talk. It takes a long time for that reason; it is supposed to take a long time, as long as it takes. Absent a professional class of politicians, or judges, or witnesses, each and every one of us will be asked to provide the central right to which every democratic citizen is entitled: review of his or her case by a jury of peers. *Peers*, not professionals.

No one wants to be picked for service on a jury. Time away from work, and family, is burdensome. In a trial that lasts four weeks or more, the burden can be heavy. And yet, once selected, each and every juror with whom I had the honor to serve demonstrated a kind of moral seriousness and professionalism that genuinely inspired me. Aghast as I have become at the behavior of many in our professional classes of politicians, financiers, and police, my faith in the simpler and nobler virtues of democratic citizens was greatly increased through this experience. I know very little about the political and the religious commitments of my fellow jurors, though in some cases I could probably make some educated guesses. It was another set of commitments that proved to be important, commitments we shared equally, and that was the key.

Placing that key in the lock of some doors that have long needed to be opened is the primary purpose for my putting this story to print.

21. See Robert C. Pirro, *The Politics of Tragedy and Democratic Citizenship* (New York: Continuum, 2011).

2

Jury Selection

IT ALL STARTED INNOCUOUSLY enough, as it does for everyone: a nonde-script, computer-generated card was delivered to my home address, indi-cating the day and time at which I was required to present myself at the Fulton County Superior Courthouse for jury duty. On a brilliantly clear Friday morning I made my way slowly down Center Avenue to the large and somewhat antiseptic courthouse building, then unwillingly abandoned the cool Southland sunshine for the dim interior of glass and steel. The line was long, as there were only two scanners and X-ray machines in opera-tion—yet one more reminder of the vast, nationwide security apparatus left in the wake of the September 11th attacks some years before.

These security measures had a more proximate cause, however: in March 2005, a man named Brian Nichols made a daring escape from this same facility after seizing the weapon of one court officer and using it to shoot and kill three persons in the course of his escape. Nichols had been brought here on charges of raping and kidnapping his then-girlfriend; a Superior Court Judge, Roland Barnes, was among the victims of this courtroom shooting. Clearly, we were all entering a violent place, one in which weapons could be seen everywhere, though nominally reserved for a certain class of persons, persons primarily assigned responsibility for the enforcement of the law. As we debate with renewed moral urgency the re-lationship between gun ownership and security or safety, such cases should remain in the forefront of our thinking. It is not so simple as believing that more guns in the right hands means more security or safety.

Nearly everyone entering at 8:00 a.m. had been called, like me, to a different duty: jury service. Witnesses and other officers of the court tended to come a bit later than we did. I now remember both the place and process as imposing, though it is remarkable to me how quickly I grew used to it all. I would pass through these same scanners almost every day for the next six weeks, ushered to the front of the line on most mornings once our case began to be heard.

What impresses itself upon me now is the degree to which we are all creatures of habit, and how easily we can be habituated into some very unusual circumstances. I grew used to the machines and scanners, used to the guns and the uniforms and the barked orders; I even grew used to some extraordinarily terrible stories—all in a surprisingly short period of time. Learning how to stay awake, morally awake, in such a condition is the challenge. And that, as I would soon discover—with the eloquent assistance of fourteen of my fellow jurors—is the most sacred responsibility we all possess as democratic citizens.

The first morning of jury service was strange from the outset; there was nothing with which I could compare it in any of my previous terms of service. After screening the video linking modern jury service to sunny old Athens and the responsibilities of democratic citizenship that were allegedly first enunciated there, literally hundreds of us were assembled together on one side of an enormous waiting room. After a brief introduction explaining the nature and severity of the case for which we were being considered as jurors, each of us was given an extensive questionnaire several pages long. We had to provide personal contact information, of course, and then we were asked a number of questions about our knowledge of, or involvement with, the police shooting of an elderly woman in the city of Atlanta, and the local protests that took place near her home on Neal Street in the following weeks.

And that was it. After completing the forms, we were told that we were free to go, and that we would be contacted again if we were still under consideration for service on this trial.

I received a phone call one week later indicating that I was indeed still under consideration, and so I was called back to the courthouse for further discussion on Monday, April 21, 2008. I was assigned to a panel (Panel 2–42), as well as given a personal number nine digits long. And then I did what most citizens called for jury duty do: I waited. I waited until the early afternoon, at which point I explained to the court that I had an appointment at my university and would need to leave in order to meet it. I had been informed that I would be finished that day around noon, so the court accommodated my schedule and reset my interview for the following afternoon. On Tuesday, April 22, 2008, at approximately 2:30 p.m., I first met several of the personalities who would so directly determine what consumed most of my time and emotional energy over the next month.

The interview, such as it was, lasted no more than half an hour. The prosecuting attorney, Peter Odum, a district attorney for Fulton County in the State of Georgia, did most of the talking. He was dressed fairly casually, a fact that clashed with his rather severe demeanor. He did not seem particularly interested in what I did for a living (as is probably clear from the introduction, I am a university professor in a department of comparative religion with a specialization in ancient Greek archaeology, history, religion, and culture), except insofar as he was interested to know what my work schedule would be like in the coming weeks. I indicated that the semester was coming to an end the very next week, and that I customarily traveled to Rome to work in the Vatican Secret Archives, normally from late May through mid-July. I had not yet purchased my tickets, I said, but planned to travel in late May; he assured me that the trial would be concluded well before that time.

If not particularly interested in the finer points of comparative religion, Mr. Odum was very interested to know how I might respond to certain hypothetical situations that apparently I would confront if seated on this jury.

Could I listen objectively to the testimony of someone who had admitted to doing other bad things? (That was easy. As a teacher, I regularly find myself in the company of students who have failed to live up to their responsibilities in a previous class, but this cannot and should not affect how I approach them in a new semester, in a new classroom setting.)

Could I be impartial when confronted with evidence about an unrelated crime to which such a confessed wrongdoer had not confessed? (That was a bit more complicated. It is a central feature of Greek ethical thought after Aristotle that a just person can do unjust things. One act of injustice does not render you ethically suspect across the board. That said, moral character matters, and characters who have developed the habits of bad action tend to be more likely to engage in them repeatedly.)

Did I have a predisposition, either positive or negative, concerning police officers? (As I have already indicated in the introduction, I feel the same way about lawyers as I feel about the police. It's a cultural commonplace to be suspicious of them, until you need them. I have had marvelous experiences with uncommonly thoughtful and dignified and courageous police officers; I have also had terrible experiences with armed police who behave in a manner suggesting that they believe they are beyond account and who act with the impunity that belief invites. There's simply no way to generalize about a class of people as diverse as that.)

Mr. Odum thanked me for my answers and for my attempts to be both thorough and honest; he seemed altogether sincere, and I would come to admire him as a remarkably thoughtful and decent man, a man who was clearly outraged by what had been done to a citizen of the county and the state he was called to protect and defend. We met in the jury room briefly when the trial finally ended, and it was especially moving to me to see him smile. He had been holding a lot back, clearly. So had we all.

The defense attorney, Mr. William McKenney, provided a fascinating counterpoint to Mr. Odum in almost every way. He smiled easily and often; he made me smile too. Impeccably dressed in a dark pinstripe tailored to fit, with a brilliant shock of greying hair and a small mustache, he was as breezy in conversation as he was elegant in self-presentation. He had a likeable way of approaching the podium with a yellow legal pad in one hand and a pen in the other. He asked short, clipped questions, almost always requiring a simple yes or no, and he made a point to thank the witness for each and every answer. With time I grew to admire him—and to like him as well.

But there was no time here. He laughingly asked me what a professor of comparative religion does, and whether it was anything like what Indiana Jones did. I laughed too, explained briefly what I did, and still do, and confessed to wishing I were more like Indiana Jones. And that was it. It seemed pretty clear that he was not seriously interested in my service in this case. Obviously I am not as astute a judge of character as I believed myself to be. If he were interested in my service, then what Mr. McKenney succeeded in doing in the space of two short minutes was to make me like him. I still do, and as I say, I grew to admire his elegance and intelligence and quiet grace more and more as this difficult trial unfolded.

I was instructed to return to the courthouse the next day, Wednesday, April 23rd, when the actual process of jury selection took place. It was a surreal process to witness, and one of the strangest rituals in which I've ever participated. We had been winnowed down to roughly seventy-five prospective jurors, all of us seated in the audience section of the courtroom. The attorneys were seated at their respective tables, but facing away from the judge's bench, looking directly at us instead. The prosecutors had large boxes of materials on the table and at their feet; Mr. McKenney had his trusty yellow legal pad. But no one said a word. Instead, the two sides passed notes back and forth to one another, apparently horse-trading, suggesting potential jurors, rejecting others. This went on silently for over an hour, and I watched it all, transfixed. What were they saying to one another? What mattered to them? How would they decide, in the end?

After roughly an hour and a half of this wordless drama, we were informed that the jury had been selected. As jurors' names were called, we were told to take our belongings, leave the audience section, and take our seats in the jury box. *We were being made into a jury.* One by one, names were called. Each time the selected juror quietly groaned, rose to his or her feet, and took the ten to twenty steps that literally turned us into a different kind of citizen. Each time a name was called, those of us not called shifted a bit more easily on our benches; we were that much closer to being released. Fourteen names had been called, and one remained (we were to be twelve jurors, plus three alternates). That last name was mine. I do not remember what I felt when my name was called, though I do remember groaning about it. I don't remember the walk at all, but I distinctly remember taking my seat in the jury box. We were raised slightly above ground level, seated in a boxed area set aside specially for us, and I had been brought into the fold, made one of them. It was a powerful experience and it left a powerful impression, one marked indelibly in my mind to this day.

It was a bit of a surprise for me to have been selected, especially in such a high-profile and volatile case as this one obviously was. Normally, I was told, being a professor and having more than one lawyer in the family was sure grounds for dismissal. No one wants a smarty-pants on a jury, not even an Indiana Jones type; it is part of the wise-man-versus-wise-guy paradox I mentioned in the introduction. It seems to me now that another factor was probably determinative in selecting this jury. This was a case with very high visibility in which television cameras were present at all times (though they were not permitted to film the jurors). The trial could not begin until every juror was present and accounted for. What the prosecution and defense needed most was the assurance that we would show up, every day, on time. That is no trivial accomplishment. Day in and day out, for several long weeks, every single one of us was seated in the jury room well before 9:00 a.m. when the court customarily reconvened. No one was *ever* late.

That is a lot easier to write, or to read, than it is to do. In the late spring when this trial took place, we the jury were composed of several students studying for final exams, as well as professors preparing them and grading them. It was clear that several of my fellow jurors were in the habit of going to their offices in the very early morning hours to deal with the myriad things that could not wait, in order to make it to the courthouse before the trial resumed. Several jurors were juggling complicated child care logistics. I made my way to my office most evenings after the trial concluded for the day, since I was in the thick of preparing a tenure and promotion file that had to include evidence of everything I had done professionally in the past eighteen years, and that had to be mailed to external reviewers in mid-June. No one ever complained about any of this; they simply did what needed to be done to meet their civic obligations in this unusual and important way.

Mercifully, we were given one week to get our work and other affairs in order, and convened again as a jury on Tuesday, April 29, 2008. We spent some time getting to know each other, as well as receiving detailed instructions on our responsibilities—the importance of punctuality, most of all—from the sergeant who would be with us every day and who cared for us almost like a mother hen cares for chicks in a dangerous world where someone has inadvertently left the door of the coop open. In the first days of the trial, we were required to meet together at a parking lot near the Atlanta Braves baseball stadium, Turner Field, and were taken together to the courthouse in a police van. I'll never forget the second day of the trial when the officer sent to deliver us went around the van with a sort of scanner to ensure that there was not a bomb on the undercarriage of the van. We looked at each other in utter disbelief. Two days later, rejecting the self-created drama of such things, the sergeant smilingly informed us that we could each make our own way to the courthouse from now on. I liked him enormously.

The trial began on Monday, May 5, 2008, quite promptly at 9:00 a.m. The jury issued its verdict on Tuesday, May 20, 2008, at 3:30 p.m. Since he had been found guilty on one of the three charges, Arthur Tesler was sentenced on Thursday, May 22, 2008, at a little before noon. The judge invited us to return for that sentencing hearing, and three of us did so. I departed for Rome on Sunday afternoon, the first of June.

3

The First Day

THE ENTIRE COURT, THE lawyers included, rose to their feet each time we the jury entered or left the courtroom. This was a powerful symbol to me, a powerful reminder of the daunting responsibility, as well as the power and authority, we possessed as the duly appointed representatives of the ultimate power in any democratic arrangement: we, the people. We were called, in a way quite distinct from the division of labor assigned to prosecuting attorneys, defense attorneys, and judges, to represent the sound judgment and deliberative skills of a democratic people long schooled by the habits of careful deliberation, the free exchange of sometimes difficult ideas, and holding one another accountable for what we say and what we do.

What had been *done* in this case, that was the test.

The presiding judge began by offering his instructions to the jury. The role of the advocates for the two opposing sides was pretty clear—each had a case to make. The judge emphasized that *his* primary purpose was to instruct us about the laws relevant to this case; in practice, he spent far more time ruling on objections made by one side or the other, decisions he rendered almost casually, but in a way that made clear how engaged he was in every turn this case took—his powers of concentration were very impressive. He emphasized that it was *our* job as a jury to evaluate the facts as presented to us, and what *we* deemed their relevance to be. It was also our duty to determine the relative truthfulness or falsehood of the testimony as presented by various witnesses. This all-important division of labor—between judges, attorneys, and jurors—would become a matter of some importance when this jury deliberated at the end of this case.

The three charges that the State of Georgia was bringing against Arthur Tesler, and for which he had been indicted, were the following:

1. that he violated the Oath of Office he swore on the evening of November 21, 2006, when Kathryn Johnston was killed;[1]

2. that he made false statements to the FBI regarding an alleged "controlled buy" he had witnessed earlier that same day, prior to the application for the fatal no-knock warrant that resulted in Ms. Johnston's death;[2]

3. that he falsely imprisoned Ms. Johnston by guarding the back door of the house when the rest of his narcotics team stormed the front door, after which they shot and killed her.[3]

It was a strange-sounding set of charges, and a serious one. Violating an Oath of Office is one thing, but lying to the FBI as part of a deliberate cover-up of prior wrongdoing is something else again. That seemed like the most serious charge of the three to me, at the time. The meaning of the third charge was not immediately clear to me, but of course we had not heard any evidence yet.

The opening arguments in the case immediately followed that Monday morning, May 5th. The prosecution's case was introduced, not by Peter Odum, the man who had interviewed me the previous week, but rather by Ms. Kellie Hill, who appeared to be the lead prosecutor in the case. It

---

1. *Official Code of Georgia 16–10–1. Violation of oath by a public officer.*
   Any public officer who willfully and intentionally violates the terms of his oath as prescribed by law shall, upon conviction thereof, be punished by imprisonment for not less than one nor more than five years.

2. *Official Code of Georgia 16–10–20. False statements and writings, concealment of facts, and fraudulent documents in matters within jurisdiction of state or political subdivisions.*
   A person who knowingly and willfully falsifies, conceals, or covers up by any trick, scheme, or device a material fact; makes a false, fictitious, or fraudulent statement or representation; or makes or uses any false writing or document, knowing the same to contain any false, fictitious, or fraudulent statement or entry, in any matter within the jurisdiction of any department or agency of state government or of the government of any county, city, or other political subdivision of this state shall, upon conviction thereof, be punished by a fine of not more than $1,000.00 or by imprisonment for not less than one nor more than five years, or both.

3. *Official Code of Georgia 16–15–42. False imprisonment under color of legal process.*
   When the arrest, confinement, or detention of a person by warrant, mandate, or process is manifestly illegal and shows malice and oppression, an officer issuing or knowingly and maliciously executing the same shall, upon conviction thereof, be removed from office and punished by imprisonment for not less than one nor more than ten years.

was difficult not to be mindful of the complexity of race and ethnicity in America during this trial, which was being heard just a stone's throw from Dr. Martin Luther King Jr.'s gravesite and the Center for Nonviolent Social Change that bears his name. A team of three white narcotics officers had been charged with falsely applying for a search warrant that resulted in the death of an elderly African-American woman. Of the fifteen jurors, only two were African-American, both of them women. As is so often the case in the criminal justice system in the United States, race was inescapable, and yet very difficult to describe or manage. In the very careful choreography of the case the prosecution presented, it was clear that they were trying to manage it; each decision, whether to have Mr. Odum (a white man) or Ms. Hill (an African-American woman) direct the questioning, was studied and deliberate. Yet I honestly could not make out the reasons for one or the other directing the questions.

It took time for me to warm to Ms. Hill. If Mr. Odum was somewhat severe in demeanor and difficult to connect with emotionally, Ms. Hill was fiery, passionate, and clearly outraged by this case. That was easy enough to understand. The facts that were not in dispute *were* outrageous, and the killing of an elderly woman in her ninety-second year based on a whole series of falsifications is the kind of thing before which the heart and the mind stand equally mute. Her outrage on behalf of Ms. Johnston I understood very well; her outrage at Mr. Tesler I did not yet share. As she attempted to put her case, I was reminded that this man was innocent until *proven* guilty, and that *reasoning* my way to that kind of conclusion would be more a matter of the head than of the heart.

Ms. Hill opted to appeal strictly to the heart. She began by playing the recorded sound of thirty-nine separate gunshots, one at a time, and then showed us an endearing picture of Kathryn Johnston. I was unimpressed and unmoved by what seemed like pointless moralizing to me. Even before hearing the evidence, I knew that Ms. Johnston's killing would not have sounded like that; rather, thirty-nine rounds would have exploded almost simultaneously from a number of different guns, all in a matter of seconds. To my mind, that sound would have been even more powerful, a kind of aural assault even more horrible to confront. But none of this said anything about Arthur Tesler. It simply reiterated what I already knew: that Ms. Johnston's death was a tragedy, for all of us.

The prosecution's case was very simple, in Ms. Hill's presentation of it: these three men were "dirty cops," period. They lied to get the original search warrant; they kept this fact from their fellow officers; they planted evidence in the home after Ms. Johnston was killed; and they engaged in an even more extensive cover-up when the FBI investigation began. The three men worked together, from beginning to end. Two of them had already confessed; now it was Arthur Tesler's turn, and he had refused to do so.

William McKenney, impeccably dressed as ever, approached us affably enough, made a point of thanking us for our time and our service, and offered a very simple counter to the story we had just heard. It amounted to a headcount at the outset: there were *two* dirty cops in this case, not three. An officer named "J. R." Smith was primarily to blame for this egregious killing; another officer, named Gregg Junnier, was equally guilty of the falsifications and the cover-up. Arthur Tesler, Mr. McKenney suggested to us, was framed by his superior officers. Naturally, this story resonated with me; it directly echoed the first murder trial I'd ever encountered in the transcripts my father had sent to me at summer camp, ages ago. Only this time the perpetrators were not members of a motorcycle gang; they were the police.

Innocent until proven guilty—this was not going to be simple. And it was clearly going to be very emotional, no matter how hard I endeavored to maintain some critical intellectual distance from the thing.

4

Policing by the Numbers, or, "Nine and Two"

I HAVE DEBATED—GIVEN MY general remove in space and time from the events of this trial that so consumed me in the late spring of 2008, and given the emotional distance that time's passing provides all on its own—how best to describe the way the story the prosecutors endeavored to tell unfolded before us as a jury. It seems important to present the case as the prosecution did, in the order they selected.

By contrast, the defense's case was very simple and comparatively brief: the task was to cast doubt on the relevant details of the prosecution's case. Most of that occurred during cross-examination. Mr. McKenney later placed Arthur Tesler on the stand for most of an entire day, and he tried to explain himself while the prosecutors tried to eviscerate his story.

Innocent until proven guilty: this was the prosecution's case, and its duty to make it stick.

That said, I do think it is important to be honest in acknowledging that I am writing this retrospectively, and that I have a much clearer sense now of what I think this case was ultimately about. So it is important to establish certain intellectual signposts along the way, to underline what seemed to me, and still seems to me, some of the more frightening implications that this case possesses for anyone who is serious about our common life and about the responsibilities of democratic citizenship in a modern democratic society.

AA

The first witness the Prosecution called to the stand was AA, a somewhat bumbling character at first glance who nonetheless grew on me as his brief testimony progressed. He was then with the Personnel Unit of the Atlanta Police Department, and his purpose was clearly to portray Arthur Tesler as guilty of the first charge of violating his Oath of Office.

To that end, AA showed us the actual Oath of Office of the Atlanta Police Department, and documents confirming that Arthur Tesler swore that oath on April 21, 2000. We would hear nothing further about the Oath of Office in this trial, presumably because the prosecutors believed this was the one slam dunk among the three charges. "Dirty hands," pretty much by definition, are evidence that one has violated any oath that promises faithful service, honor, and compassion. This is as true for a soldier who tortures as it is for a police officer who kills without cause. Tesler's failures on all three counts were clear to the prosecution, though not yet to us. Thus, the lion's share of the prosecution's case was devoted to convincing us that Arthur Tesler, just like his two partners, was "dirty," and hence responsible both for the death of Ms. Johnston and the elaborate cover-up that followed.

As things turned out, the first charge about the Oath of Office was not quite the slam dunk the prosecution believed it to be, and that had everything to do with the wording of the original indictment. The charge was not that Tesler had violated his oath in general, but that he had done so specifically on the night of November 21, 2006. I am a teacher, and so the importance of care and forethought in written expression is very clear to me. The first of many failures on the prosecution's side lay here, in the sloppy word choice and imprecise reasoning in the charges brought against Mr. Tesler at trial.

BB

The second witness the prosecution called was to begin making the substantive case against Arthur Tesler by explaining in greater detail what he was alleged to have done. To put that story in a context, we needed to know how the Atlanta Police Department worked, first of all, and more specifically how the narcotics unit was structured; that was the story we began to see assembled now.

Lieutenant BB was a quietly compelling person, visibly very nervous, which seemed strange for one as senior in the Atlanta Police Department hierarchy as she was. She drank a great deal of water during her testimony—pretty much continually, while she spoke—and this clearly had a lot more to do with nerves than with hydration. Still, I found her quiet, decent, and trustworthy, at least in general and at least at first.

She had served in the Atlanta Police Department for seventeen years and was then working with the Office of Professional Standards (OPS). Previously she had been a criminal investigator in Zone 5, but had been promoted to the post of narcotics unit commander (where she served for nearly two years). As we soon learned, this meant that the whole thing had happened on her watch, so to speak—small wonder that she was nervous.

The prosecution wished to use her as a source of general information about the structure of the Atlanta Police Department's Narcotics Unit, and what the main tasks were for officers under her command. The defense attorney naturally would use her to get more specific information about those same structures of policing—things we would have been better off not knowing, from the prosecution's point of view.

The lieutenant was asked first about the training police officers receive in applying for and then serving search warrants. She indicated that everyone at the police academy received thorough training in the protocols of search warrants because—and this was the last thing she said to the prosecuting attorney—serving a search warrant is among the most dangerous things police officers ever do. I never forgot that point; we the people never should.

Next, the lieutenant was asked about the general chain of command in the Atlanta Police Department. She described the structure as follows:

- Chief of Police
- Assistant Chief of Police
- Deputy Chief
- Major
- Lieutenant
- Sergeant
- Senior Patrol Officers or Investigators
- Police Officer (this last was the rank with which you entered the Atlanta Police Department after completing training at the police academy.)

A few points of clarification about this command structure followed. If persons share the same rank, there are no relevant chains of command or obligations to obey orders. Even within the strict rules of the command structure, the lieutenant assured us, any officer is always free to make an anonymous complaint. Clearly, the prosecution was suggesting that Arthur Tesler should have done so.

The lieutenant was asked next about three specific terminological distinctions:

1. *Found drugs*, we were told, is the term used to describe drugs of any kind that cannot be linked to a specific person and must therefore be submitted for processing and destruction.

2. *Confidential Reliable Informants*, or CRIs, are persons who are loosely kept in the employ of the Atlanta Police Department. They had all been ID-processed, were interviewed on a fairly regular basis, were paid for these services, and their information was deemed to be far more reliable than testimony received from a person under investigation or arrest.

3. A *controlled buy* involved a narcotics unit arranging for one of their paid informants to enter a house where drugs were believed to be held and distributed, and to purchase a relatively small amount, normally in the range of $50. The informant would confirm the presence of larger quantities of drugs in the house, and this evidence could then be used to request a search warrant to investigate the home. Any controlled buy involving more than $500 would need to be approved by officers overseeing the narcotics unit investigators.

The lieutenant was also asked about the specific structure of the narcotics unit of the Atlanta Police Department. She was in charge of that unit, and there were two sergeants working directly under her supervision. Each sergeant was the leader of an eight-person team of narcotics investigators. There were only two teams in Atlanta, which divided responsibility for policing all six of the zones into which the city of Atlanta had been divided (Team 1 handled Zones 1, 2, and 4; Team 2 handled Zones 3, 5, and 6). That strange administrative tick proved important later on: at one time there may have been as many as six teams responsible for narcotics policing in Atlanta; budget cuts had reduced the force from six units to two.

Team 1 was the team involved in the tragic killing of Ms. Johnston in 2006; it was led by Sergeant W. S., who supervised the activities of the following eight investigators. I have abbreviated the names of most of these officers (excepting Officers Tesler, Junnier, and Smith) to protect their anonymity; I have marked with an asterisk the names of those officers whose testimony we heard during the trial, and grouped them into the ad hoc teams-within-the-team that seemed to establish who worked with whom on a near-daily basis.

- C. B. (male)
- H. B. (female)

- Gregg Junnier (a white male)*
- J. R. Smith (a white male)
- Arthur Tesler (a white male)*

- G. S. (a black male)*
- M. G. (a black male)*
- N. L. (a black male)

Arthur Tesler, we were told, was the youngest man on Team 1, as well as the youngest officer in the entire narcotics unit; he had only been serving for nine or ten months on the evening that Ms. Johnston was killed.

The last general point of order that the lieutenant was asked about concerned two men who would become central to this trial and to this story: Alex White, who had been a Confidential Reliable Informant; and Fabian Sheats, who was arrested by Officers Junnier, Smith, and Tesler and was used as a decidedly *less* reliable source of information on that fateful day in November 2006. The testimony of both men, the lieutenant insisted, would have required verification for a search warrant application.

Finally, the prosecution asked the lieutenant to describe her own involvement in the tragic events of November 21, 2006. There wasn't much to tell. She saw the three officers at the Atlanta Police Department firing range in the morning. She next saw Arthur Tesler that evening at the Neal Street crime scene; she indicated that she did not discuss what had happened with him then, since the Homicide Division was required to take over the investigation after a narcotics shooting.

Lieutenant BB did talk to J. R. Smith later at the hospital (as I noted, three of the officers who stormed Ms. Johnston's home were injured by their own ricocheting bullets), and she asked him for the details concerning the search warrant, since she had not known about it. This seemed remarkable to me: how could the person in charge of two teams of narcotics investigators not even know that one of those teams was serving a search warrant, and an especially dangerous one at that? The oversight of these two teams, and the far more informal units within them, appeared to be negligible. But this had a great deal to do with how increasingly overworked this skeleton crew of narcotics officers had become.

Officer J. R. Smith informed the lieutenant that they had arrested Fabian Sheats earlier in the day for selling marijuana and had taken him from the scene in Arthur Tesler's car, then picked up Alex White to make a controlled buy at the home of Sheats's supplier. The lieutenant dutifully typed up a memo to that effect. She spoke briefly to Arthur Tesler on the phone, but she did not speak to Gregg Junnier at all. The shooting took place on the Tuesday before Thanksgiving, and the FBI took over the investigation on the Monday after Thanksgiving (November 27, 2006). At that point, Gregg Junnier confessed to her that they had manufactured their original story. Arthur Tesler never approached her at all.

What the prosecution had attempted to show was that there were very clear lines of authority and very clear accountability structures in place in the narcotics unit in November 2006. But no such oversight, no matter how well intentioned, could prevent rogue officers from misbehaving in such egregious circumstances, and then misrepresenting their own misbehavior. That, the lieutenant suggested, was what had happened on November 21, 2006, and she simply was not closely enough involved with the three men to do anything more than believe their account of what had happened and to report the events to her superiors. In this case, the lieutenant had clearly been duped—by Gregg Junnier and J. R. Smith for a certainty, and implicitly by Arthur Tesler as well.

~

Mr. McKenney turned immediately to dismantling this rather rosy picture of Atlanta urban policing. He noted that the sergeant in charge was on bereavement leave when Arthur Tesler was originally assigned to Team 1 of the narcotics unit. Who, Mr. McKenney wondered, was in charge when a sergeant was absent? Traditionally, the senior member of the team, the lieutenant answered; in this instance, that would have been Gregg Junnier.

How would a young officer such as Arthur Tesler be integrated into the team? I began to wonder. As we were to learn later on, there was no really organized way of doing so. The investigators on both teams essentially worked together in whatever informal ways they saw fit. The smaller arrangements were all informal and impromptu; the only time the team worked together at full force was when serving a search warrant. It was unsurprising in these circumstances, I suppose, that these teams would self-segregate into smaller units divided by race, and that was what seemed to have happened on Team 1.

Arthur Tesler eventually fell in with Officers Junnier and Smith, with results that were to be disastrous for him and for the entire Narcotics Division. The only special training police officers received prior to joining the narcotics unit involved weapons training and the proper use of CRIs. The rest of it they were expected to pick up by observing their superiors. Clearly, Arthur Tesler had apprenticed himself to some unfortunate professional role models.

Mr. McKenney then turned to the details of the evening of November 21, 2006, just prior to the storming of Ms. Johnston's home on Neal Street. When an entire team was assembled for such an event, a briefing was required to bring the entire team up to speed on the situation they were about to confront. The officer who applied for the search warrant was considered the lead officer, and he or she was responsible for the briefing. In this case, the lead officer was J. R. Smith.

In general, at such a briefing, the main concerns were the following, according to the lieutenant: Were there guns at the house? Dogs? Surveillance equipment? And where was the precise location of the drugs in question? Mr. McKenney then asked if it would be weird to have an informant present at such a briefing. (Apparently, as we would learn later, Fabian Sheats was still in Arthur Tesler's car during the briefing). He wondered also if it would be weird to call someone away from a briefing. (Tesler himself would later contend that he was on his cell phone when J. R. Smith gave what amounted to a fatally short briefing).

Mr. McKenney paused and smiled, assuring the nervous lieutenant that he had just a few final points he wanted clarified. They involved some further police terminology—terminology not previously mentioned by the prosecution. The first term was *insurance drugs*, a special class of found drugs that were allegedly held back in order to be planted at some future crime scene. The second term was *padding*, the practice of skimming off extra money that was intended for use by CRIs to make a controlled buy. Naturally, while the lieutenant was *familiar* with such terms in theory, she insisted that these were not acceptable practices for the Atlanta Narcotics Unit.

Mr. McKenney had just one question more. Had the lieutenant ever heard of the phrase "nine and two"? She claimed that she had not, but *every* lower-level police officer whose testimony we heard later in this trial could tell us in detail what the phrase meant. This phrase concerned the monthly assessment that all narcotics investigators undergo. It was the name for an alleged quota system, setting a benchmark for each investigator to make at least nine arrests and to apply for at least two search warrants every month.

I was appalled. Just by doing the math, a terrifying picture was beginning to emerge. An entire narcotics team had to be assembled to serve a search warrant. There were eight persons on each team. If each person on each team applied for *at least* two search warrants per month, that meant the team was serving *at least* sixteen search warrants every month. Since narcotics investigators work only twenty days a month, they were expected to be involved in the most dangerous single aspect of their job *at least* 80 percent of the time they are on duty. Suddenly, the Atlanta Police Department, with its quantitative system of assessment and oversight, was on trial, not just Arthur Tesler. The whole system was designed to create danger. The eventual killing of someone like Ms. Johnston in something like these terrible circumstances was beginning to seem like a foregone conclusion.

This was all going to be much more challenging than I had anticipated. And painful.

5

The "War on Drugs"

I BEGIN THIS CHAPTER with a brief summary of the testimony of the first three witnesses we heard from next, and then I intend to take a much closer look at the fourth (this last witness was one of three or four witnesses around which the entire case would prove to revolve).

CC

CC was an instantly likeable guy with a big face, a big smile, an attractive bundle of high energy, and the biggest biceps I believed I had ever seen. He had served on the Atlanta Police Department for twenty-one years, eleven of them with an eight-person canine unit. Thus he knew everyone in the narcotics unit, including Arthur Tesler, Gregg Junnier, and J. R. Smith. He lived next door to Arthur Tesler, in fact.

CC was scheduled to work a 10 a.m. to 6 p.m. shift on November 21, 2006; the day would last much later than that, in the end. He was patrolling on Lanier Street at roughly 2:20 p.m. when he came upon Officers Smith, Junnier, and Tesler, who had apparently just come upon a cache of found drugs. The four men did a further sweep of the area but found nothing else. CC agreed to stay and to continue the survey of the area with his dog, and he was told to expect another phone call from Gregg Junnier (a call that never came).

CC was back in the police station when a call came in after 6:00 p.m.; he proceeded directly to 933 Neal Street. Upon arriving, he saw that Gregg Junnier had been shot. He also saw the sergeant for Team 1 and J. R. Smith, the latter of whom had blood on his face and seemed entirely unaware of it. The scene was chaotic and had not yet been secured; CC stayed on site until nearly midnight. He never saw Arthur Tesler at the scene.

Another canine officer, EE, eventually was assigned to oversee the search of the premises, so CC had little information about what was actually found there. He had heard, however, that the three officers (Junnier, Smith, and Tesler) had made an arrest elsewhere, earlier in the day. He testified that he had a bad feeling about the Neal Street scene, and not just due to the shootings and general chaos. He indicated that he was already concerned that drugs may have been planted in the house.

Earlier in the day, when these same three officers first arrived on Lanier Street in a marked police car, they obviously would have driven off anyone who was associated with the found drugs they confiscated. J. R. Smith told CC that they had discovered one pound of marijuana in total, but did not show it to him. He indicated that he'd found it quite by accident when he went behind a tree in the woods surrounding the apartment complex to urinate. The canines found nothing more at the scene, nor did a later search called in by Gregg Junnier.

CC had worked often with J. R. Smith and Gregg Junnier, who were the senior officers in this informal gang of three, but he had not interacted directly with Arthur Tesler. He had never entertained doubts about the men's integrity until that day, but when he discussed the day's events with EE later that evening, grave doubts began to arise for them both.

DD

DD (who also shared his street name with us) seemed a sad figure to me, a bit disheveled, and subject to some physical ticks that made it seem as if he were not quite at home in his own skin. He had lived in this area for eighteen years and had worked as a Confidential Reliable Informant (CRI) for the Atlanta Police Department since 2006. He was generally paid between $30 and $100 for information that led to confiscation of stashes of marijuana and cocaine as well as any related arrests.

November 21, 2006, just so happened to be his last day as a CRI for the Atlanta Police Department; he'd worked as an informant for nearly two years, using the money to supplement the money he made wiring homes. In November 2006, J. R. Smith was the narcotics investigator with whom he worked most closely; they had each other's phone numbers and kept in relatively close contact.

DD called J. R. Smith at 4:06 p.m. to report that a man he knew only as Fabian was selling crack cocaine in the Green Store parking lot on Samson Street. DD described him as most easily identified by the gold jacket he was wearing. The man in question was leaving the Green Store, moving very fast away from the parking lot, when the three police officers arrived. DD indicated that he had to call J. R. Smith several times before he was finally paid for this tip, the last one he ever called in to the Atlanta Narcotics Unit—and surely the most tragic of them all.

DD also recalled that he had never purchased drugs of any kind on Neal Street before. Dealers will often pay homeowners to sell drugs out of their yard, he observed, something he also told the FBI when they interviewed him. "Controlled buys" were one type of activity in which he had been involved, but he indicated that J. R. Smith had also called upon him to make other kinds of purchases. He occasionally saw Arthur Tesler with Gregg Junnier and J. R. Smith at such times, but normally Tesler remained in the office. The tragic base of this testimony was that DD's final tip to the Atlanta Police Department was to set in motion a sad chain of events that led to Ms. Johnston's death later that same day.

EE

EE was a cool, seasoned professional woman who exuded a kind of quiet confidence. She seemed honest, direct, a very sound person. She had worked for fourteen years with the RED DOG ("Run Every Drug Dealer Out of Georgia") Canine Unit. She brought a picture of her dog, "K-9 Chad," who had been trained by her six years before. Such a dog normally works with only one trainer, she informed us; K-9 Chad was a highly trained and award-winning police dog, a fact of which EE was clearly very proud.

On November 21, 2006, EE began her shift at 4:00 p.m. She was dispatched to the Green Store location at approximately 4:30 p.m., and arrived there fifteen to twenty minutes later. When she arrived, J. R. Smith directed her elsewhere to conduct her search; she and K-9 Chad soon found some small bags of marijuana (some blue plastic, others clear). They subsequently found more bags containing both marijuana and crack cocaine; this time the marijuana was in clear and orange bags, whereas the cocaine was all contained in clear bags. EE gave the first recoveries to J. R. Smith, who placed them in his car, whereas the remaining finds were given to another Canine Unit officer, TT. Officer EE noted that Arthur Tesler remained in the police cruiser throughout this process, accompanying an unidentified figure in the back seat.

Later that same day, EE received a call for assistance at around 6:15 or 6:30 p.m. She arrived at the Neal Street address five minutes later, but was not instructed to perform a canine search of the premises until approximately 2:00 a.m. After an extensive search that concluded in the basement of the house, EE and K-9 Chad finally turned up three small bags of marijuana; there were other narcotics investigators present when this discovery was made.

The next day, while preparing her report, EE called Arthur Tesler at 1:16 p.m. in order to find out the total amount of the found drugs secured on Simpson Street that he and his two fellow officers had made earlier on the previous day. After consulting with Gregg Junnier by telephone, Arthur Tesler called back at 1:30 p.m. to confirm that there were fifty-eight grams of marijuana in total, but that the crack cocaine had proved to be "flex" (a street term for fakeries).

Thus the Canine Unit had discovered three separate caches of drugs on that one day: the marijuana that EE had given to J. R. Smith; the crack cocaine that she had given to the Canine Unit's officer TT; and the marijuana that was discovered at 933 Neal Street late that evening (Arthur Tesler and Gregg Junnier were no longer at the address, but she recalled that J. R. Smith had stayed on while the search progressed). She recalled that the basement was very cluttered, dirty and difficult to reach; she thought it seemed a very odd place to hide drugs, and noted that it was a nearly impossible place from which to exit the premises. The whole site seemed strange, as she later indicated to her colleague, CC.

Fabian Sheats

Fabian Sheats came into the courtroom shackled at the hands and feet, and that made him seem initially quite sympathetic to me. With a big, round face, he seemed like he was just a kid, though in fact he was twenty-five years old. By the end of his testimony, I was convinced that he was a complete and total manipulator, much smarter than he appeared to be, and that he had been playing everyone, probably for years. He had been making a living by selling drugs since he was seventeen years old, and was then serving three weeks in the Fulton County jail on an open charge. His lawyer was present in the courtroom, though no deal had yet been made with the district attorney.

Fabian Sheats was arrested for possession of marijuana with intent to distribute on November 21, 2006. Those charges were dismissed in exchange for his cooperation in this case. The deal hinged on his providing truthful testimony, on committing no further offenses, and on the successful prosecution of this case.[1] By that standard, he had reneged on his deal three times, as far as I was concerned, playing Peter to the prosecution's Christ.

Arthur Tesler had previously arrested Fabian Sheats—twice. Gregg Junnier and J. R. Smith were with him on both occasions. Every time he saw them they were working together. On November 21, 2006, the day that ruined [his] life, Fabian Sheats went to the Green Store between 3:00 p.m. and 4:00 p.m. to sell crack cocaine (not marijuana, as was alleged and charged). He testified that he was dressed in a gold coat, a white shirt with blue jeans, and Timberland boots. When the three officers arrived in their car and moved to grab him, he placed the remaining drugs in his mouth, and later swallowed the bag, at which point he recalled that Arthur Tesler slammed his head against a guardrail. The three narcotics investigators called in the Canine Unit at that point. Arthur Tesler detained two more persons in the area, Gregg Junnier was in the driver's seat, and J. R. Smith accompanied the Canine Unit on its search of the premises. After they found and collected the drugs, J. R. Smith returned to the police car and began taking more drugs out of his pockets.

At this point, Fabian Sheats claims that he confessed falsely to owning the marijuana; his motive for doing so was that he already had two outstanding charges for crack cocaine. Arthur Tesler was outside the vehicle

---

1. I was told that I must have misunderstood this last point. I recall it as a detail that struck me at the time; that does not mean that I am correct. It is one more important reminder about how human and imperfect this process was, and how imperfect I was in the role I played. The text of Mr. Sheats's Cooperation Agreement [State's Exhibit #21, dated November 30, 2006] is in Volume IX of the trial transcripts. There is one interesting phrase: "The District Attorney's office agrees to consider whether it will make a specific recommendation to the Court that Mr. Sheats should receive a sentence reduction in consideration of his cooperation." Clearly, Sheats was committing himself to play an essential role in any successful prosecution. And the District Attorney's office was determined to be coy in agreeing to help him subsequently, but there was no requirement of successful prosecution. It was striking that Gregg Junnier seemed equally ambivalent about whether successful prosecution was a condition for him to receive a reduced sentence. He initially seemed to suggest that it was (Volume XI, page 61), then later insisted stridently that it was a matter of indifference to him whether Arthur Tesler was found guilty or not (Volume XI, pages 97 and 137).

at this point, letting the two other suspects whom he had detained go. He then returned to the police unit and began filling out the arrest paperwork.

The three investigators drove Fabian Sheats to the Marquette Club parking lot. They counted out fifty-five bags (or roughly seven grams) of marijuana. Gregg Junnier was still driving, with Arthur Tesler in the passenger seat. J. R. Smith was in the back seat with Mr. Sheats. They waited for approximately forty-five minutes, during which time Mr. Sheats indicated that the cocaine he had ingested began to affect him.

After J. R. Smith received a call on his cell phone, the four men drove to the Fulton County jail. They had made no effort to organize a controlled buy of any kind. After a brief discussion, J. R. Smith left the vehicle and entered the jail. Mr. Sheats recalled hearing Officers Junnier and Tesler make a bet about how long J. R. Smith would be gone; he estimated that it was fifteen minutes in total. When Gregg Junnier made the observation "that was quick," J. R. Smith indicated that when he entered the jail, "she [the judge] came up on the screen, and gave it [the search warrant] to me."

The four men left the jail and drove to a fire station; *en route*, the three officers were discussing the need to "make a buy." A black van, and more police canine units, arrived soon after Junnier, Smith, and Tesler did. Mr. Sheats recalled seeing three narcotics officers, other masked police officers, and a canine unit. Left in the car in handcuffs, Mr. Sheats watched them talk for roughly ten minutes. The officers then placed him in the black van in restraints; Tesler and Junnier followed the van in their patrol car.

Mr. Sheats reported being left alone in the van when he heard "a lot" of gunshots, then the shrill of sirens, cries of "officer down," then sheer chaos. After approximately one half hour, a police officer opened and closed the door of the van. Roughly fifteen minutes later Mr. Sheats was taken away in a minivan. It was then, he testified, that he saw the house for the first time.

Clearly, Mr. Sheats' testimony was important—and just as clearly, he was lying. But in which parts? He was trying to protect himself, that much was clear. And Mr. McKenney was trying to protect Arthur Tesler. To that end, Mr. McKenney first asked Mr. Sheats why, when he was later questioned by the Office of Professional Standards, he did not mention that Arthur Tesler had hit him on the head. It was Greg Junnier who had handcuffed him, after all, not Arthur Tesler.

Mr. McKenney proceeded to hammer away at his credibility by noting that Mr. Sheats had been arrested three times before: for drugs and robbery in 2002, for violent robbery in 2003, and for a firearms violation in 2004.

Each time he was arrested, Mr. Sheats pled guilty (presumably to avoid being labeled a "recidivist" and thereby receiving the maximum penalty). Since this arrest in 2006, and the deal to which he agreed, Mr. Sheats had been arrested two more times for cocaine possession: in April 2007 and again in March 2008. The charges currently facing him would thus be his "third strike"—and the symbolic end of his sad, bad road. He indicated that he was aware that the deal he had made with the district attorney's office (never specified to us) did not automatically exempt him from prosecution. Mr. McKenney's purpose seemed to be to sow "reasonable doubt" about the entirety of Fabian Sheats's story.

The prosecuting attorneys elected to cross-examine Mr. Sheats briefly again when Mr. McKenney had finished with him. They seemed to be concerned with three fairly simple matters. Mr. Sheats was interviewed twice by the Atlanta Police Department's Office of Internal Affairs. During the first interview, on the day after the shooting (November 22, 2006), he was naturally only asked about the shooting itself. Four days later (on November 26, 2006), he offered a much fuller report of the entire day's events; it was then that he complained specifically about Arthur Tesler. He entered into an agreement for his testimony and cooperation four days after that (on November 30, 2006); hence he had complained about these narcotics investigators being corrupt *before* he was ever offered a deal.

A much more complicated picture was beginning to emerge, to my eye. By declaring a "war" on drugs, a number of unintended consequences had resulted. First, the refusal to make any meaningful distinction between relatively benign drugs, like marijuana or hallucinogenic mushrooms, and those drugs that are clearly dangerous and destructive, like heroin or crack cocaine, had produced an untenable situation for everyone involved. The narcotics unit was being asked to focus its very limited energies and resources far too broadly, everywhere at once. One drug bled into another. Bags of marijuana and crack cocaine were confused with one another or even substituted one for another. It scarcely seemed to matter what drug Fabian Sheats was alleged to have been selling when he was arrested. Far more disturbing, if it were true, was the implication that J. R. Smith had taken three bags of found drugs from the trunk of his car and planted them in Ms. Johnston's basement, where EE and K-9 Chad later found them. It was as if J. R. Smith believed, in retrospect, that three small bags of marijuana would justify the issuance of a no-knock warrant and the killing of an innocent ninety-two-year-old woman. Drugs were drugs, after all. Something was out of joint.

Second, the three-strikes-and-you're-out laws were not reducing drug activity or the amount of drugs available on Atlanta's streets. Not at all. What they were doing was giving regrettable actors like Fabian Sheats every incentive to lie, to give the police precisely the information he knew they wanted, and then to lie again in enhancing his story. Mr. Sheats was as directly involved in the death of Ms. Johnston as J. R. Smith had been.

Third, everyone who was involved on the drug-dealing side of this story had been a black male. Much has been written to demonstrate how our increasingly aggressive drug laws are enforced disproportionately against relatively young black men.[2] Surely there were white men and women in the city of Atlanta who were addicted to crack cocaine; we would never meet one in this trial. The Atlanta Police Department has made admirable strides in becoming a more integrated community of public servants; prisons in the State of Georgia, however, continue to be as racially lopsided as any single social arena promoted and policed by the state.[3]

Gradually, the hypocrisies and overt moralizing of North American society were being placed on trial, not just a corrupting administrative police structure or a corrupt police officer. And this trial was becoming more emotionally exhausting by the day.

2. See Michelle Alexander, *The New Jim Crow: Mass Incarceration in the Age of Colorblindness* (New York: New Press, 2010) esp. 58–94, 173–76, and Vanessa Barker, *The Politics of Imprisonment: How the Democratic Process Shapes the Way America Punishes Offenders* (New York: Oxford University Press, 2009) 13–15, 18–19, 143–67, 183–85.

3. On September 15, 2012, the *Atlanta Journal Constitution* reported on Mayor Kasim Reed's new initiative to increase the Atlanta Police Department to its highest-ever level of 2000 officers; disturbing questions about the suitability of many recruits were raised by that article. Here once again the assessment has been quantitative, not qualitative. Wikipedia reports a striking ethno-racial breakdown on the current Atlanta police force: 57% African-American, 41% White; 1% Hispanic and 1% Asian.

According to the U.S. Department of Justice's Bureau of Justice Statistics (utilizing data assembled in 2009), there were 1,619,395 inmates serving prison sentences in federal and state facilities, or one half of one percent of the national population. These persons were overwhelmingly male (for example, 52,598 men and 3,634 women in the State of Georgia). The State of Georgia did not count persons serving time in local jails awaiting transfer, so the State's actual numbers are assuredly higher. The Federal Report did not break down ethno-racial statistics state-by-state. Nationwide, in 2009, black men were incarcerated at a staggering rate seven times higher than whites. Of an estimated 1,446,000 sentenced inmates in December 2010, there were an estimated 561,400 black men incarcerated, versus 451,600 white men (by contrast, an estimated 48,000 white women were incarcerated, versus 26,600 black women). These figures are indicative of a policing regime well described as "the New Jim Crow."

6

New Technologies and the New Policing

FF

FF was an enormously likeable and self-styled "computer geek" who was earnest and engaging and who clearly wanted to help. At the time he served as the Clerk of Court for Fulton County. He had been called to the stand to explain a relatively new electronic system that police officers could use to apply for search warrants. The Electronic Warrant System (EWS) had been established in 2002 and was designed to expedite the issuance of both arrest warrants and search warrants.

Prior to the development of this system, all requests had to be made by the sponsoring officer (who was normally called the "affiant" in this trial), either over the telephone or in person. This new computerized system enabled police officers to apply for a search warrant much more expeditiously by utilizing the interactive functions that most all computers now possess.

The way it works is this. A police officer, like J. R. Smith in the case before us, may enter the computer bank at the Fulton County jail to log in to the search warrant system. He brings a small thumb drive or other diskette with him, a diskette that has the generic information for a search warrant already filled in. He simply needs to change the relevant details of the case—the date, the address, the names of the suspect(s) (if known), and the name of the Confidential Reliable Informant or other witnesses who have corroborated the presence of the evidence or the suspect(s) the police wish to secure and/or detain. This is done interactively via interactive chat (and may now be supplemented with a video link), and because the system is entirely electronic, there is a permanent log of the process available on the generic hard drive (the "S: Drive") for the Fulton County computer system.

FF walked us through the log for J. R. Smith's search warrant request on November 21, 2006. Warrant Case Number E001XXX indicated that J. R. Smith logged in at 5:36:22 p.m. (he was identified by his operator's identification). There was a back-and-forth discussion of the request until 5:49 p.m. Judge GG signed off on the search warrant request at 5:53:52 p.m., and granted the officers permission to enter the house without identifying themselves beforehand. This is a so-called no-knock warrant, an even more dangerous kind of warrant to serve. J. R. Smith logged off at 5:55:41 p.m.

The speed of the whole transaction was uncanny—and terrifying to consider. Fabian Sheats was arrested at roughly 4:30 p.m. The Canine Unit found drugs at the scene roughly one half hour later. One half hour after that, J. R. Smith was already at the Fulton County jail, requesting permission to break into a private residence unannounced. He presumably lifted a generic warrant application from his thumb drive, added the address Fabian Sheats had given him, probably retained information about a controlled buy using the name of his previous CRI, discussed the case with a judge for ten minutes at most, and a search warrant was issued four minutes later. He left the Fulton County jail just before 6:00 p.m. Less than one half hour after that, Ms. Kathryn Johnston was dead. The entire situation unfolded in no more than two hours. The speed—which is to say, the lack of time for reflection—was striking to me, but there was another detail that nagged at me as well. CC, a member of the Canine Unit whose testimony we had already heard, mentioned that he was working a 10 a.m. to 6 p.m. shift on November 21, 2006. Was this judge on a similar schedule? Had she hurriedly signed off on a search warrant just five minutes before her shift ended and it was time for her to go home?

GG

Judge GG was a most impressive woman who exuded an air of quiet authority. She seemed exceedingly self-confident overall, and was emphatic in testifying that she was known to be a stickler for the rules. What was striking to me immediately was the way in which her demeanor suggested that she could only imagine herself as being called here to help us, to provide us with specialized information we could not know otherwise. It simply did not register (as it so clearly had with Lieutenant BB) that she might be questioned about her own role in this case, or that she had not been sufficiently careful, sufficiently vigilant, in issuing the warrant that resulted in Ms. Johnston's death. I do not blame her for what happened so soon thereafter, but I am tracking a very old story, I suppose: the person who is most assured of his or her moral clarity may be tempted by that assurance to act unclearly. It happened to the Athenian democracy; it happens to most all of us. Such a person will tend to have a very clear, and therefore very simplistic, sense of what went wrong here: a "dirty cop" lied to me. What the judge never seemed to imagine was the possibility that she might have sniffed out the lie. If Fabian Sheats was arrested at 4:30 p.m., and the three officers left the crime scene after 5:00 p.m., then how could there possibly have been enough time to arrange a controlled buy at that address? The officer of record was sitting at his computer in the Fulton County jail just one half hour after leaving the original crime scene. Even I saw that, admittedly in tragic retrospect. Much depended on the specifics of the lies J. R. Smith fabricated in his original warrant application (we were later to learn that J. R. Smith had mentioned a man named "Sam" who was alleged to have been seen by the CRI at 933 Neal Street, along with one kilo of cocaine).

GG had been a practicing attorney since 1981. She became a magistrate judge in Fulton County in 1996, after fifteen years as a practicing attorney. She thus offered us a unique and compelling glimpse into the structure of her legal mind, by walking us through how she understood the Fourth Amendment protection against "searches and seizures" without "probable cause."

In order to maintain the protection of a citizen's constitutional rights, in this judge's judgment, the application for a search warrant needs to provide a description of who is making the request, the specific reasons for the request, and what they may reasonably expect to find at the location in question. But this judge went further; *probable cause* for granting permission to enter a private home is a very big deal, she assured us, and therefore requires a lot more than simply the "reasonable expectation" that you will discover something at the address. That is what controlled buys and other eyewitness informants are designed to provide. And it is important to note that, in addition to the online *application* form, the officer making the request is also required to file an *affidavit*, which is a sworn statement under oath (this is why they are referred to as affiants).

Judge GG had signed search warrants for J. R. Smith, Gregg Junnier, and Arthur Tesler before; she recalled that they often worked together. They knew what she required in any such application: reliable informants; evidence of a controlled buy at the location; a clear and concise description of the person being sought; a description of the address; a description of the crime or crimes expected to be found at the location; and a qualified affiant. Clearly, she said, this warrant application met all of these criteria.

In addition, the judge deemed a no-knock warrant advisable only if 1) drugs may otherwise be destroyed at the scene, or 2) the officers serving the warrant may be in particular danger. A police officer can request a no-knock warrant, or a judge may recommend one; in this case, she recalled that J. R. Smith requested a no-knock warrant due to the alleged presence of surveillance cameras at the location. Judge GG indicated that she granted this request out of concern for the officers' safety, not for fear of losing the cocaine. That seemed both reasonable and important, further evidence of the extent of J. R. Smith's original lies.

Judge GG admitted that much of the material in such an application is boilerplate, easily called up off a floppy or thumb drive. J. R. Smith's credentials, for instance, were laid out in detail; so was the history of his work with Arthur Tesler. There was no reason to reproduce that information anew each time. But the case details were different, and the details were what mattered to her. She insisted that she was known to have very high standards—and a very high threshold to meet before granting requests for search warrants.

As I mentioned at the beginning when I described the initial selection of the jury, we were fifteen jurors in total, not the customary fourteen. I assumed that this was due to the high profile the case enjoyed, as well as to the fact that the trial promised to be a long one. Jurors can get sick, or called away due to family emergencies. But this created one strange situation every day. There were now only fourteen seats in the jury box, so one of us was always seated in a separate chair slightly outside of the jury box, at ground level and much closer to the witness stand. Early in Judge GG's testimony, we were required to take a break so that the lawyers could discuss a matter with the presiding judge. While they did so, Judge GG began talking to the juror who was seated in the hot seat, joking and wondering why he'd been seated apart from the rest of us. It was a small thing in a way, but the presiding judge, clearly bothered by it, actually interrupted his conversation with the lawyers and turned to his fellow judge to remind her that talking to individual jurors was not permitted in a court of law . . .

As I've said, it is a very old story: the person who is most assured of his or her moral clarity may be tempted by that assurance to act unclearly. And that messy fact had tragic consequences.

7

"We're All in This Together"

WE HAD BEEN DANCING around the central agents in this trial for some time, playing around the periphery, as it were. We had now reached the point where we needed to meet the other members of Narcotics Unit Team One—men, as we would soon learn, whose lives had been altered by the shattering events of that awful night. All of them clearly felt implicated, and even responsible to varying degrees, for the tragic death of a nonagenarian who lived alone and who was clearly the kind of citizen they were commissioned to serve and protect. Their failure to protect her from harm weighed heavily on the minds of two African-American members of that team who had not worked closely with Officers Junnier, Smith, and Tesler, and who could not have known that the search warrant was bogus. Much to my surprise, Ms. Johnston's death weighed still more heavily on the mind of Gregg Junnier himself. Junnier's testimony, in particular, was burned into my mind at the time; it remains so, to this day. But it will take some time to get to it.

M. G.

M. G. was handsome, young looking and athletic, talented and soft-spoken. He was far and away the most compelling person we had heard from to that point. He had worked with the Atlanta Police Department for nine years, serving for six as a patrolman with a street beat in Zone 6, then a patrol car in Little Five Points, then a bicycle patrol in East Atlanta. He later became a detective and was assigned to the narcotics unit. He left the unit briefly, then returned to work as a member of Team 1 under Sergeant W. S. in 2004.

He was placed on administrative leave in the immediate aftermath of the November 21st shooting but had been able to work unrestrictedly since then.

Officer M. G. worked primarily with his fellow officer G. S. as an undercover detective. By contrast, Arthur Tesler worked in police uniform and in a marked police car. Officer M. G. could not easily make arrests without blowing his cover, whereas Officer Tesler and his company could. As a result, he "made" far fewer cases. One wondered how he was assessed at the end of each month.

Officer M. G. was out on a normal street patrol on November 21, 2006; he returned to his office in City Hall East at around 1:00 p.m. He testified that he was the only one in the office then, as most of the rest of his team were at the firing range. He later received the call to serve a search warrant, but when he did, he knew nothing more about it. He left the office with Officer N. L. in an undercover car, roughly fifteen minutes after everyone else had left. These two men were thus the last to reach the fire station where the pre-raid briefing was held.

When they arrived, J. R. Smith was already conducting the briefing, as was his responsibility as the applicant/affiant. Officer M. G. observed that J. R. Smith was usually very thorough with his briefings, but was notably less so on this occasion. Officer M. G. vaguely recalled the mention of someone named Sam, of cameras stationed around the perimeter of the residence, and the confirmed presence of one kilo of cocaine inside. (According to Lieutenant BB's testimony, one kilo of cocaine had an estimated street value of $20,000.) The patrol car and black van arrived at the location five minutes later. Officer M. G. traveled in the van with Officers G. S., N. L., J. R. Smith, and Fabian Sheats; he wore a mask so that Fabian Sheats would not be able to identify him later on.

At this point in his testimony, Officer M. G. became very emotional, so we took a break before continuing. Juror or no, and all of my moral outrage aside, my heart went out to him. There were a lot of victims in this case.

When we resumed, Officer M. G. ticked off the relevant details of the raid. There were burglar bars on Ms. Johnston's front door, and it took nearly a minute to cut through them with a halogen device. Naturally, this eliminated the surprise of a no-knock warrant, and, unbeknownst to the police, Ms. Johnston had been roused from her bedroom and had taken out an old six-shot revolver she owned. Officer M. G. had the battering ram, so as soon as the door was opened, he found himself standing immediately before a shadowy figure holding a gun. He bolted, and leaped off the front porch. He heard many shots fired as he did so.

Ms. Johnston was in the doorway, barely breathing, when he returned. He left the house again in order to examine his partner, Officer G. S., who had been wounded in the leg by a ricochet. The interior door to the basement of the house was locked, so Officer M. G. went around to the back of the house to enter that way. They used the halogen device to pry open that doorway as well, and once inside, he observed a great deal of dirt and clutter, but no drug paraphernalia. Naturally, a large number of police officers showed up almost immediately.

G. S., C. B., and Gregg Junnier, the three officers who had been shot, were all taken to the hospital for treatment. Officer M. G. visited them there, then returned to his office at City Hall East, and later went home. He was subject to counseling and investigative interviews the next day. He learned roughly one month later that the warrant they had served at 933 Neal Street was bogus.

~

In his cross-examination, Mr. McKenney began by asking for clarification about some of the details of the raid. Officer M. G. had also been working on a case involving one kilo of cocaine that day when he was called away to serve this search warrant. He observed Fabian Sheats in the parking lot and so, in order to protect his anonymity, he drove around the block and phoned his colleagues, who placed Fabian Sheats in the van. When he entered the van, he asked Mr. Sheats if there were guns at the location; Sheats said there were not because "Sam" was a convicted felon and was not permitted to own a gun.

There was no real tactical plan, Officer M. G. explained, so everyone took up their usual positions. Arthur Tesler was placed at the back of the house because "he was the rookie"; his job was to secure the perimeter and thus to ensure that no one tried to run away from the back of the house. The task, Officer M. G. suggested, was "to contain and detain." There was no evidence in this case that anyone was ever in the basement, nor that anyone ever tried to get out of the house. Naturally, this was important because the third charge against Arthur Tesler was that he had "falsely imprisoned" Ms. Johnston by holding her in the house. According to the details we were hearing, that seemed like a stretch.[1]

1. I am no longer convinced that this was so. The wording of the law that Arthur Tesler was accused of violating reads as follows: "Official Code of Georgia 16–15–42.

Mr. McKenney then turned to the administrative structure of Team One. Officer M. G. confirmed that, after Sergeant W. S., Gregg Junnier was the senior officer on the team. This normally meant that when the sergeant was absent, Officer Junnier would direct team activity, drive the cars, and so on. Officer M. G. indicated that he had his own suspicions about Alex White as a CRI; he seemed "too comfortable, too relaxed," and much too close to the three officers with whom he worked most closely. He also recalled that he never heard about a controlled buy being made at 933 Neal Street, and that Fabian Sheats was present and had heard J. R. Smith's briefing. No narcotics officer received special training in serving warrants, he indicated, not even the no-knock warrants that were so commonly used among them.

Mr. McKenney turned finally to what was beginning to seem like the central question in this case. Was Officer M. G. familiar with the term "nine and two"? He was. This was the unwritten monthly benchmark whereby officers on his team were expected to make nine arrests and apply for two search warrants, every month. There were ways around the rule, Officer M. G. observed. For instance, you could receive credit for a search warrant if you wrote the report, even if you had not sworn the original affidavit.

The prosecutors asked a few pointed questions in their redirect examination. While Officer M. G. had indicated that he did not know where Arthur Tesler was during the briefing, he could confirm that he was not inside the van. He also admitted that Arthur Tesler was "the rookie guy," the junior member of Team 1, not a genuine rookie. In that sense, Gregg Junnier had no technical seniority over him; only the sergeant did, and Sergeant W. S. was indeed present at this raid. So Tesler would not have been subject to orders from his colleagues, Junnier and Smith.

As for the "nine and two" rule, it named a standard that was rarely met. Officer M. G. himself, as an undercover agent, rarely met it and had suffered no consequences as a result.

False imprisonment under color of legal process.

When the arrest, confinement, or detention of a person by warrant, mandate, or process is manifestly illegal and shows malice and oppression, an officer issuing or knowingly and maliciously executing the same shall, upon conviction thereof, be removed from office and punished by imprisonment for not less than one nor more than ten years."

The district attorneys were alleging that Arthur Tesler, along with Gregg Junnier and J. R. Smith, was indeed a police "officer issuing or knowingly and maliciously executing" a "manifestly illegal" search warrant.

G. S.

G. S. was a very big guy with a close beard; he too seemed deeply sensitive and thoughtful, however incongruous this appeared, given his size. After six years in the U.S. Army, Officer G. S. joined the Atlanta Police Department and had served for fifteen years. He started out in the Special Enforcement Division, then worked as a foot patrolman in Zone 5, then served briefly with the RED DOG Canine Unit. He had been a narcotics investigator for three years (2003–2006) when the shooting occurred. He was still on administrative leave due to the Neal Street shooting but had never been charged with anything.

Officer G. S. gave us a candid and thoughtful glimpse into how informal partnerships within the team were formed, unformed, and reformed; things, he said, "just came together." Officer G. S. worked mostly with M. G. and N. L.; he was senior to them, but without authority over them. They tended to work together in the mornings, then dealt with team activities (like serving search warrants) in the afternoons.

As he recalled, Arthur Tesler had originally worked most closely with Officers C. B. and H. B. Officer C. B. had worked with Gregg Junnier for a while, until Junnier started patrolling more with J. R. Smith. H. B. and Arthur Tesler were the latest additions to Team 1, and while H. B. began working mostly with officers M. G., N. L., and himself, she later paired off with C. B. She was on vacation in November 2006. Arthur Tesler, while initially involved more with Officers C. B. and H. B., eventually cast his lot with Gregg Junnier and J. R. Smith, and in some important ways that decision sealed his fate.

On November 21, 2006, most of Team One was at the firing range in the morning, for at least an hour. After his training, Officer G. S. had a meeting with his Confidential Reliable Informant, since he was then cultivating a relationship with two suspected drug dealers. He went to lunch, then returned to City Hall East. He never entered the building, but remained in the parking lot because he was informed that they were going straight out to serve a search warrant that J. R. Smith and Gregg Junnier had secured. Such warrants were referred to as "paper."

At this point, Officer G. S. choked up visibly and confessed that he hated "ratting out" a peer. Police officers, he said, are "family." For the second time, we were witnessing the emotional cost police officers themselves had paid for this awful ordeal. But unlike Officer M. G., Officer G. S. expressed as much concern for his fellow officers as for Ms. Johnston.

Officer G. S. traveled in the raid van with Sergeant W. S. and Officer C. B. Officers Tesler, Smith, and Junnier, along with Fabian Sheats, were in a patrol car. Officers M. G. and N. L. were in an undercover car. The sergeant was visibly angry, Officer G. S. recalled; he was monitoring the anticipated delivery of one kilo of cocaine on that same day, and this warrant had interrupted his own case. He was openly angry with Gregg Junnier when they gathered at the fire station.

During the briefing, Officer G. S. was in the van with Fabian Sheats. J. R. Smith was in the doorway. Arthur Tesler and Gregg Junnier were close to him. Officer G. S. recalled a relatively thorough briefing: the affidavit was read out loud; the no-knock status was emphasized; the officers were told to expect to find a large amount of cocaine in the house; mention was also made of the presence of surveillance cameras and a suspect named "Sam"; they were told that a controlled buy had been made earlier in the day.

Officer G. S.'s assignment was to carry "the shield," behind which the officers storming the front door would gather. Arthur Tesler was stationed at the back perimeter. Greg Junnier was in the lead. When Officer G. S. placed his shield on the windowsill, he recalled noticing the absence of cameras where he had expected to see them. Officers Junnier, Smith, and M. G. worked on the burglar bars, thereby forfeiting the element of surprise, so they announced themselves.

Once successfully past the burglar bars, M. G. rammed the door, and Officer G. S. entered with the shield. He was scarcely two feet inside the home when he saw a person in the shadows to his right holding a gun. He heard a shot, then fired his weapon; he assumed that he shot Ms. Johnston. A number of other shots were fired immediately; Officer G. S. heard that his fellows had been hit, and so he moved to the door with his shield, to protect the team. That was when he felt a burning in his leg, continued to the right, saw a body on floor, and kicked the gun away. He observed that Ms. Johnston was still alive at that time. He handed Officer M. G. the shield and left the house.

Officer G. S. had been shot in the right leg and buttock. Officers Junnier and C. B. had also been shot. All three were taken to Grady Hospital in downtown Atlanta for treatment. While there, Officer G. S. recalled a nurse screaming at him, calling him a murderer; he believed that he was improperly treated as a result, and his leg eventually became infected. He was placed on administrative leave, called Officers Tesler, Smith, and Junnier to follow up, but never received a reply from them.

～

Mr. McKenney, it seemed to me, had located the singular point of entry into this heartfelt testimony: the notion that police officers are a family, and that it is an act of disloyalty to make a complaint against a family member. Indeed, the first thing we learned under cross-examination was that the prosecutors in this case had first suspected him of homicide when this case broke and, ironically enough, served a search warrant at his own home. Officer G. S. understood their reasoning, bore no grudge, and trusted them nonetheless. He truly seemed to be a company man.

Officer G. S. noted that it is rare to get a search warrant without a controlled buy but that it can be done, depending on the quality of other information. This is all at the discretion of the affiant, in this case J. R. Smith. It would not be a partner's job to question this, not even a senior team member like Gregg Junnier.

Officer G. S. also recalled that Fabian Sheats heard the briefing, but he did not find that unusual at the time. He distinctly recalled J. R. Smith reading from the search warrant, since that was protocol. He also recalled that Gregg Junnier had a habit of running in ahead of the shield, in what he called "go-go-go mode." Fellow officers *had* complained about this, and Sergeant W. S. had communicated this concern to Officer Junnier himself. Arthur Tesler, Officer G. S. observed, was assigned to be the perimeter man, because he was the newest member of Team One.

As for "nine and two," that rule was known to everyone, including their sergeant. It was an unwritten rule, but then, seniority itself was an unwritten rule. Clearly, Officer G. S. obeyed rules, even the unwritten ones, and he expected others to do so as well. Amazingly, when asked a few follow-up questions by the prosecutors, his last word was that he had never been misled by Arthur Tesler and that he trusted him still to this day.

I wanted to share his *esprit de corps*, but we were about to get a very different description of the hidden realities in this strange sort of semi-secret family.

Gregg Junnier[2]

Gregg Junnier entered the courtroom shackled in irons at the hands and feet, and I nearly gasped. We all did. He looked like one of the prisoners one sees in photographs of the liberation of the Nazi camps. Skeletal and

2. His stunning and dramatic testimony may be found in Volumes X and XI of the trial transcripts: Volume X, pages 118–267; and Volume XI, pages 8–141.

unimaginably pale, he appeared to be in the throes of chemotherapy, or else dying of grief. It seemed to be the latter; he informed us that he had lost forty pounds in the previous twelve months. Still more striking, he was not asking for our pity by reporting this; it was just the way things were now.

In 2006, Officer Junnier was an eighteen-year veteran of the Atlanta Police Department. He had first served as a patrol officer in Zone 5 for ten years, then moved to investigations for a year, then landed in the narcotics unit; he had worked as a narcotics investigator for eight years when the shooting took place. He retired from the narcotics unit on January 1, 2007, just prior to his arrest.

At the time of his retirement from the force, Gregg Junnier was being held on federal charges (conspiracy to violate civil rights) as well as on state charges (mainly the homicide). He pled guilty to voluntary manslaughter; he was represented by counsel then and he still was. Officer Junnier confessed to firing his weapon inside Ms. Johnston's home on the night of November 21, 2006, though he could not say whether he had killed her; it seemed more likely that J. R. Smith had. (It seemed more likely to me, based on what I'd heard thus far, that several of these officers had shot her, including G. S. prior to his own injury). Officer Junnier had not yet been sentenced when he testified, but if he cooperated fully, he indicated, he faced ten years' imprisonment on the federal charges, and an as yet undetermined sentence from the State of Georgia. He confessed to the FBI prior to making his deal with the prosecutors, though we did not learn the details of the conversation or the deal.

When Gregg Junnier first joined the narcotics unit in 1998, there had been five seven-man teams in Atlanta. He was assigned to Team 4, which became Team 1 under W. S. when the Atlanta Narcotics Unit was reduced from five teams to two, with the responsibility to police the entire metropolitan area. While each investigator was assigned to a particular zone, they were free to roam throughout the city. The mission of the narcotics unit in such tight budgetary circumstances, Officer Junnier suggested, was to make arrests; it scarcely mattered what kind. He indicated that he had applied for over one hundred search warrants from Judge GG alone, but never without some kind of corroborating witness testimony about the location they intended to investigate. That was one of the many things that was different about this search warrant, and this tragic case.

The conversation then turned to Alex White, a Confidential Reliable Informant whom Officer Junnier first met when he was processed by the narcotics unit under the direction of C. B. After that, Officer Junnier used

Alex White on a weekly basis. By 2006, Gregg Junnier had settled into a casual routine, working primarily with officers J. R. Smith, Arthur Tesler, C. B., and H. B. But then Officer H. B. significantly reduced her time on the street and mostly handled paperwork in the office; C. B. later left this informal partnership because he did not like J. R. Smith. That left J. R. Smith and Arthur Tesler, with whom he rode most frequently; they had a strictly working relationship, however, and did not socialize together.

Gregg Junnier proceeded to give us an uncannily detailed account of what happened on November 21, 2006, as well as the nature of the cover-up the three men attempted afterward. It made for harrowing listening at times. His day began at 10:00 a.m., and as he worked at his desk waiting for the other members of his informal team to arrive, he received orders from Sergeant W. S. to go to the firing range. He was there until roughly 1:00 p.m. with J. R. Smith and Arthur Tesler; they left the firing range and drove to Zone 1, looking to make arrests. At approximately 3:00 p.m. they arrived at 350 Lanier Street, an apartment complex known to house a lot of drug activity, mostly marijuana. Officer Junnier indicated that they were paid by the owners to watch this property; we were to learn that most of these narcotics officers, significantly overworked and underpaid, supplemented their income either by working second jobs or by doing this sort of thing. Many did both.

Upon arriving, the three men noticed that a door had been kicked in; Officers Junnier and Tesler went to investigate, while J. R. Smith remained outside policing the grounds. Officer Smith came back to the building with a sandwich bag of marijuana, which the men processed as found drugs; they called in a Canine Unit officer (CC, whose testimony we had already heard) who searched the grounds. It was during this search that J. R. Smith received a phone call from DD about drugs being sold on the street; the three men joked that it would almost surely be Fabian Sheats, and when they pulled into the Green Store parking lot, they saw that it was.

Fabians Sheats was arrested by Arthur Tesler at 4:00 p.m.; J. R. Smith went to a fenced area where the three men expected his drugs would be stashed. Gregg Junnier was in the police car and called in another Canine Unit. Fabian Sheats was complaining about Officer Tesler punching him in the mouth when J. R. Smith returned with a stash of plastic bags, a scale, and other drug paraphernalia, accusing Fabian Sheats of being their owner. When Canine Officers EE and TT arrived, they quickly discovered bags of marijuana and cocaine together at the location. Fabian Sheats confessed that the marijuana was his, but not the cocaine. The three men nonetheless arrested him for possession and intent to distribute both marijuana and cocaine, according to Officer Junnier (Sheats reported this differently, of course, for obvious reasons). As J. R. Smith left to look for more evidence, Fabian Sheats refused to talk, indicating that he "wasn't a snitch."

Officers Junnier and Tesler reminded Sheats that this would be his third strike, and so eventually he told them where he purchased his share; he indicated that it was part of a cut kilo of cocaine. Arthur Tesler wrote the arrest report, but said that the three officers had conducted surveillance prior to the arrest; that part was an unnecessary lie. In Officer Junnier's judgment, when J. R. Smith returned to the car, the three decided to pursue Fabian Sheats's tip. Sheats offered to make a semi-controlled buy for them; the three men were tempted, but decided against it. Instead, they pulled into a parking lot and started writing up his arrest report.

It was now roughly 5:00 p.m., and the time was tight. J. R. Smith continued to interrogate Fabian Sheats, probing him for information, while Gregg Junnier called Alex White to arrange a controlled buy. Mr. White indicated that he had no transportation, and so this plan fell through as well. At that point, Fabian Sheats offered to show them where the house was from which he had purchased his cocaine. When they arrived at the address, Officer Junnier remarked that Mr. Sheats hid beneath the window and acted scared; he identified the house and the three investigators debated what to do next. Should they knock on the door? Or get a search warrant? When Mr. Sheats confirmed that he had seen a kilo of cocaine on the kitchen table—a relatively large amount—Gregg Junnier concluded that they needed to arrange a controlled buy, to which J. R. Smith replied, "or not." When Officers Junnier and Tesler indicated that they would not write such a warrant, J. R. Smith told them that he would.

Gregg Junnier testified that, since he felt the responsibility for this bogus search warrant would not belong to him, he essentially ignored it. He confirmed that there was no controlled buy at the Neal Street address, and that he never called Alex White back. Tragically, Alex White called Officer Junnier back at 6:00 p.m.; Junnier dismissed the call, saying that the issue had been taken care of. Thus, even as the three men were preparing to storm Ms. Johnston's home, this all might still have been avoided had they agreed simply to confirm the presence of drugs at this address through a controlled buy.

The testimony covering the all-essential next forty-five-minute time span felt like one of those scattershot, cut-and-paste scenes in a bad crime thriller. The four men spent five minutes or more driving around Neal Street, then five more minutes to get to the Fulton County jail. It was now 5:15 p.m.

They were at the jail for roughly one half hour in total. J. R. Smith went inside to apply for the warrant. Gregg Junnier reiterated to Fabian Sheats that if they found this amount of cocaine at the location, then he would indeed be released, but if not, then he would be prosecuted. The two officers then joked among themselves about how long it would take J. R. Smith to get the warrant, since he already had all of the information on a thumb drive. While the three men were waiting in the car, Sergeant W. S. called and indicated that he was working on "something big." It was at that point that Gregg Junnier informed him that they were already at the jail applying for a search warrant to be served that same day, so the sergeant's case would have to wait. Another missed reprieve. Officer Tesler had also indicated his need to leave early that evening, since his wife had something to do and would be angry if he were late. Officer Junnier informed him that he was free to go, but Tesler indicated that he wanted to stay to see the kilo of cocaine. So many narrow misses, and seemingly inconsequential decisions. It was now 5:50 p.m.

During the seven-minute drive to the fire station, J. R. Smith handed the warrant to Officer Tesler, who looked at it briefly and returned it to him (Officer Junnier claimed that he had already indicated that he did not want to see it). J. R. Smith informed Arthur Tesler that he was mentioned in the search warrant, and also indicated that he claimed they had enlisted Alex White—"the A-Team made the buy," as he put it. By contrast, Fabian Sheats was not mentioned in the warrant application at all, which Gregg Junnier found odd. (I did not; Fabian Sheats wasn't on Smith's thumb drive, but Alex White was). It was approaching 6:00 p.m.

When Sergeant W. S. arrived, he questioned Fabian Sheats himself about the location and warned him that "there better be dope there." He was angry because he had been forced to drop the search for his own kilo of cocaine, but Officer Junnier recalled that he became excited about this tip when he heard Sheats's description of the location. It took ten minutes or more for Officers M. G. and N. L. to arrive. J. R. Smith conducted the briefing, assigning everyone, including the sergeant, their positions. Gregg Junnier was in the lead; as the rookie, Arthur Tesler was assigned to the rear perimeter. It was shortly after 6:00 p.m.

When they arrived at the house, things did not look right, according to Junnier's strong recollection. He said as much to J. R. Smith and asked him what he wanted to do. "Hit it," was the reply. It took the team one and a half minutes to pry open the burglar bars. The inside door was locked, so Officer Junnier called for the ram. He immediately saw a figure in the doorway who appeared to be a bald man with a gun, and then he saw a flash of light.

Officer Junnier fell backward down the stairs, was injured, half-emptied his magazine and reloaded; when he got up, he saw that Officer G. S. was still shooting, and that Officer M. G. had disappeared. When the team sergeant arrived from the back of the house, he saw that several officers had been hit, and ordered the rest back into the house to clear the location. Officer G. S. had the shield; Officers Junnier, J. R. Smith, C. B., and the team sergeant were lined up behind him (Officers M. G. and N. L. were still missing). It was then that Officer Junnier saw Kathryn Johnston on the floor, gasping for breath; inexplicably, he said the sergeant ordered that she be handcuffed. This grotesque detail did not register with me until much later. It was 6:36 p.m.

Officers Junnier and J. R. Smith swiftly cleared the house, but did not notice the basement door; there were no signs of drug activity at all. J. R. Smith asked him what they should do; Junnier replied that they had best hope there were drugs somewhere in the house. It was then, adrenaline fading, that he realized he had been shot in the chest, leg, and face. He was taken away in an ambulance with Officer G. S., whose injuries were mild, and Officer C. B., whose injuries were more severe. They were taken to Grady Hospital, where J. R. Smith and Arthur Tesler arrived two hours later.

Already concerned with the cover-up, J. R. Smith was irritated that Junnier had not answered his cell phone. J. R. Smith and Arthur Tesler then related the cover story they had come up with: that they indeed took Alex White to make a controlled buy in their patrol car (a detail Junnier found ridiculous) or else in Arthur Tesler's car (a detail he found less so). Junnier asked if drugs had been found at the Neal Street location, and Tesler nodded affirmatively. J. R. Smith worried that the drugs might not be found, because there was not much to find. When Junnier was released from the hospital and returned to City Hall East, he spoke with J. R. Smith and Arthur Tesler on the phone again. They indicated that they had called Alex White and that everything was in order, relatively speaking. They were still in this together.

When Gregg Junnier returned to his office the next day, J. R. Smith was already giving his statement to the homicide investigators. Arthur Tesler informed him that the team sergeant was already dubious about the alleged controlled buy. Nonetheless, Officer Junnier told the homicide investigators that he had indeed driven officers Tesler and Smith to meet their CRI and to make a controlled buy. Lieutenant BB got involved at this stage and wanted to find out more about "Sam." Meanwhile, J. R. Smith was actively trying to catch up with Alex White in order to pay him for some outstanding work he had previously done for them, buying his silent assent to their story. Later, when Alex White kept calling the three men, Gregg Junnier arranged for him to receive $100 more; he directed J. R. Smith to take the money to Alex White on Thanksgiving Day. The cost of a human life seemed uncommonly cheap.

Gregg Junnier testified that the three officers met on five separate occasions to coordinate the details of their cover-up. The first meeting was called by Arthur Tesler at a pizzeria he liked; he simply wanted to clarify and confirm the details of the story as related in J. R. Smith's original warrant application. Gregg Junnier called the next meeting, when a news story broke about the search warrant allegedly being bogus (as we were to learn, Alex White had gone to Fox 5 News by then). Arthur Tesler called the third meeting, to set up the next false story about the surveillance he mentioned in his own arrest report for Fabian Sheats. The paper trail of lies that had multiplied in the course of a single afternoon was becoming increasingly difficult to manage, Junnier observed.

Arthur Tesler called yet another meeting after his interview with the FBI (while he claimed he felt good about it, Gregg Junnier thought he had already turned on them, and J. R. Smith was in a panic because the Police Benevolent Association had informed him that they would no longer represent him). Arthur Tesler called a fifth and final meeting with Gregg Junnier alone; he mentioned that his wife was pregnant, and it appeared to Gregg Junnier that he had decided to tell the FBI the truth. He claimed that he supported Officer Tesler in that decision.

The last hour of questioning had been excruciatingly slow. This seemed intentional on the prosecutors' part. We ended at 5:15 p.m., and thus we had all night to think about this story before Mr. McKenney could ask any questions about it. I did think about it. All night. And it was then that the image of Ms. Johnston, handcuffed and dying, finally registered with me.

~

This had been damning testimony for Arthur Tesler. Mr. McKenney was most interested in understanding why we should believe a man who had lied to the FBI about this case in the past, though he was paradoxically also interested in Gregg Junnier's descriptions of on-the-job narcotics training, and wanted confirmation of the meaning of some of the terminology we had heard before. It seemed as if Mr. McKenney wanted us to assume that Gregg Junnier was lying about Arthur Tesler's role in the cover-up, but that he remained a reliable source of information about the broader culture of corruption in the Atlanta Narcotics Unit.

As part of his plea agreement, Gregg Junnier was required to cooperate with any state or federal prosecution for which he was needed. The review of his service to the prosecutors was entirely at the state's discretion; if they were unhappy with his testimony in any way, then he was facing a life sentence without the possibility of reduction or parole. Accordingly, Mr. McKenney put the question very pointedly to him: was his job now to enable multiple successful prosecutions? Or simply to tell the truth? Mr. McKenney noted that Officer Junnier had already assisted in the conviction of Sergeant W. S., and that he had testified against N. L. Now it seemed to be Arthur Tesler's turn. Was this all part, Mr. McKenney wanted to know, of Gregg Junnier's "downward trajectory"?

Gregg Junnier admitted that he lied in his first statement to Atlanta homicide investigators shortly after the shooting on November 21, 2006. When he did so, J. R. Smith and Arthur Tesler were hovering nearby, clearly resulting in a "cross-contamination" situation that enabled the three to keep their stories straight. Officer Junnier made two statements to the FBI: the first on December 11, 2006, and the second on January 25, 2007. What, Mr. McKenney wondered, had changed? (Looking at Junnier's face, I had a strong sense of what had changed—his guilty conscience had literally consumed him). Gregg Junnier indicated that he originally thought he was protecting J. R. Smith, since he did not really think he was culpable; in the end, he thought that they had all been played and manipulated by Fabian Sheats. Later, he changed his mind about that, and concluded that it was J. R. Smith who had really manipulated both him and Arthur Tesler, drawing them into a web of deception from which neither man could extricate himself.

So the real question, Mr. McKenney suggested, is *how soon* the lies reached the point where he could no longer continue to support them? When did he stop going along with the lie and go to the FBI instead? And—more to the point—why didn't he invite Arthur Tesler to go with him? That seemed an important line of questioning to me, though no one pursued it further. It may have been as simple as the fact that Gregg Junnier believed that Arthur Tesler had already confessed to the FBI by then. It was all a bit murky, and that was the doubt Mr. McKenney clearly needed to underline for us.

Turning to the details of on-the-job narcotics training and the "when in Rome" atmosphere in which these underpaid, overworked, and hyper-assessed officers did their dangerous duties, Mr. McKenney made his points pretty effectively. Narcotics officers received only four hours of training in search warrant protocols; most of what they learned on the job came in the form of using search warrants from colleagues as templates for their own. Officer Junnier estimated that he had applied for one hundred search warrants with Alex White alone, fully 80 percent of which contained false information.

Next Mr. McKenney asked Officer Junnier to describe some of the terminology we had heard before:

1. *Insurance drugs*, he said, involved a technique that had been imported from the RED DOG Unit by J. R. Smith. It was thus not surprising that he would have planted such drugs in Ms. Johnston's home after the shooting.

2. *Padding vouchers*, he said, was a common technique used to secure quick cash. Everyone knew about it, and it was most easily justified to supplement car repairs for those officers who occasionally drove their own cars on assignments.

3. *"Nine and two"* was the key, of course: Officer Junnier described this as a very difficult standard that put enormous pressure on all involved. It was a strictly numerical system that invited shortcuts, bogus warrants, and the rest. Junnier also indicated that both of his superiors, Sergeant W. S. and Lieutenant BB, pressured junior officers to "get their numbers up" or "the unit look[ed] like shit." As a general rule, Officer Junnier liked to go up the food chain, as it were, tracing drugs back to their source, but so long as the Atlanta Police Department merely looked at the *quantity* of arrests, not their *quality*, none of this mattered—marijuana, heroin, cocaine: it made no real difference.

Perhaps the most telling detail in the cross-examination of Gregg Junnier concerned the discussion of the situation that took place at the Fulton County jail. Fabian Sheats had given them a location with a description, a named suspect with a description, and a description of the type and quantity of drugs involved. That might have been enough for a search warrant, though probably not. In general, Junnier said that J. R. Smith was known for "padding his warrants"; he liked to double, or triple, his probable cause. Why none of this was even mentioned in J. R. Smith's warrant application seemed weird to him, in retrospect. Alex White, who had never been with them, was mentioned in the application; Fabian Sheats, who had been there the whole time, was not.

But it did not seem odd at the time. At the Fulton County jail, Gregg Junnier refused to apply for the warrant, and refused to read it when J. R. Smith returned with it. Arthur Tesler declined to make the application, because he "didn't need it" (meaning that his numbers for the month were already set). Clearly, "nine and two" was the rule; and so, needing a warrant and in a hurry, J. R. Smith simply used the template on his thumb drive to apply for a generic warrant, then engaged in an assault on a private home that was not generic in any way—if such things ever are.

⁓

The single most memorable exchange came when Kellie Hill returned for a brief redirect examination of this all-important witness. I have never forgotten it; I am sure I never will.

> Q: Tell me if you need training to know the difference between the truth and a lie.
>
> A: No, I don't need training for that. . . .
>
> Q: Tell me if you need training to know the difference between right and wrong.
>
> A: I can see some cases where you might, yes.[3]

Rightly or wrongly, the whole case hinged on that distinction, I was now beginning to see. I did not yet see a way to resolve it. "Right and wrong" had come to be defined by the strange game, and the even stranger numerics, that this kind of policing was said to require.

---

3. Trial transcripts, Volume XI, page 99.

8

Breaking the Case

Alex White

ANTONIO ALEXIS WHITE, NICKNAMED Alex, was twenty-six years old when he testified before us; he lived with his mother in South Atlanta in November 2006, very close to the federal prison. He served as a police informant for four years, as an ATF informant for three years, and as a Secret Service informant for just a few months. It seemed to me a strange way to make a living, but there was something very compelling about Alex White's brash, mildly comic, and self-deprecating manner. He smiled broadly and clearly liked to laugh. But he was just as clearly a very serious man; by the time his testimony was finished, he seemed almost heroic, in his own way.

It all began in 2002, when Atlanta police detained him and searched his home. While they found no drugs on the premises, they did find a probation warrant and arrested him on that basis. He was later arrested for the possession of marijuana (he pled guilty), for the possession of cocaine (again, he pled guilty), and for criminal trespass (this charge was dismissed). Officer C. B. approached him at that time to work for the narcotics unit as a Confidential Reliable Informant. In that capacity, he had known Gregg Junnier and J. R. Smith for four years, and Arthur Tesler for nine or ten months.

Now came the complicating factor, as far as his reliability was concerned: Alex White was then up on new charges for the possession of cocaine in Douglas County, Georgia. He had an attorney for that case, and a second attorney advising him regarding his testimony about the Neal Street shooting. He originally hired an attorney, he told us, because he was afraid that he was going to be framed by the Atlanta Police Department for the cover-up of the killing of Ms. Johnston.

On November 21, 2006, Alex White called Officers C. B. and Gregg Junnier, basically looking for work. As I have said, this all seemed like a very strange way to make a living, and designed to generate arrests. In an economic crisis, even policing and prisons have become big business. At 5:05 p.m., Gregg Junnier called him and wanted to know where he was, whether he had access to a car, and whether he was available to make a controlled buy. He indicated that he was relatively far away from the officers and had no way to get to them, but that he was available to make a buy. Officer Junnier said he'd try to arrange to have a car pick him up and would call him back. At 6:00 p.m., Gregg Junnier returned the call, which Alex White missed, so White called him back. Officer Junnier seemed rushed and eager to get off the phone, which suggested to Alex White that he had already arranged what he needed.

The central facts were these: Alex White testified that he was unfamiliar with the Neal Street address (#933), that he never made a controlled buy there, and that he never saw Officers Junnier, Smith, and Tesler on the 21st of November 2006. But the most harrowing aspects of White's own story unfolded subsequently.

J. R. Smith called Alex White very late on the night of the 21st, and sounded very odd. He asked White where he was and informed him pointedly that he had made a controlled buy earlier that day at 933 Neal Street. The story would be that he approached the house, met a man named Sam at the front door, then went around to the back of the house to secure two $25 bags of crack cocaine in clear plastic bags. White recalled that J. R. Smith informed him that "we fucked up, and I need you to cover our ass." Alex White wrote that line down on a pad of paper, he told us, because he understood its seriousness. Something very bad was clearly afoot.

While he was still on the phone with J. R. Smith, another Atlanta police officer beeped in; that was how Alex White first learned that there had been a shooting death on Neal Street. Shortly thereafter, Alex White's mother called him to the television to see the breaking news story. White already wondered if these two things—J. R. Smith's panicked phone call, and this breaking news story—were connected.

Then the phone calls came in a cascade. The officer who first informed him of the shooting called him back. Then Gregg Junnier. Then J. R. Smith. Then Arthur Tesler. Then Sergeant W. S. Then "everybody." Alex White quickly learned that they were all involved in the shooting, and he wondered what he should tell to whom, since he already feared that he might be framed by police he now believed to be unscrupulous and dangerous. White eventually told his girlfriend, and an ATF agent, and other law enforcement officers, since he wanted a witness trail for his own protection. If these police officers could draw him into a situation to cover up one killing, then presumably they were capable of another.

Playing both sides of the thing with some real delicacy, Alex White talked to Gregg Junnier again while Junnier was still in the hospital being treated, then tried to reach Arthur Tesler, but never did. The next day, November 22nd, Alex White called an agent with the ATF. He informed that agent that Gregg Junnier had been shot and had called him from the hospital. He further indicated that he had been told to lie, saying he had made a controlled buy, and naturally the ATF agent was shocked by the news; other ATF officers came right away to interview Alex White.

Things were escalating, and spiraling out of White's limited control. Gregg Junnier called again to confirm the details of the bogus story that J. R. Smith had told him on the previous day. Arthur Tesler also called him and reiterated the details of this same story, and the importance of keeping them straight. Next, someone else called from City Hall East, someone Alex White did not know. The officer informed him that they wanted White to look through a photo array in order to identify "Sam."

The ATF officers had very pointedly warned Alex White not to get into any car with Atlanta Police Department officers. So Alex White made an appointment to meet the men on a very visible street corner. But when a young man from his neighborhood came close to the car, which would have blown Alex White's cover—and his livelihood, such as it was—White ducked into the back of their car so as not to be seen, and the door closed behind him; there were two officers in the front of the car.

The two men never showed him any photographs; instead, he claimed they took him to a scrap metal lot, ran him by the Neal Street address, and asked a great many questions. Alex White claimed that he feared for his life, since the Atlanta police clearly needed his help with the lie, and he no longer trusted any of them. After fifteen minutes in the car with these unknown officers, Alex White surreptitiously called an ATF agent so that the agent would be able to eavesdrop on their conversation. Finally, panicky himself and uncertain what to do, White gave up the charade.

He revealed that he was on the phone with the ATF, told the agent explicitly what was happening, and tried to get the Atlanta police officer to talk to the ATF himself. One officer left the car and, in White's opinion, merely pretended to make a call; he then informed Alex White that the ATF agents were *en route* to City Hall East, so they should go to meet them there. Since White had already been explicitly warned by the ATF not to travel with the police in their own vehicles, he suspected that this was also a lie.

Not knowing whom to trust, Alex White ran out of the car, and into the Varsity (a famous fast-food restaurant and a landmark in the city of Atlanta), then bolted across the street to a BP gas station, past some state troopers in the parking lot. He holed up in the restroom and made a 911 call. We heard the tape of that call, presented later by another state witness, and it was awful. There simply was no way to fake fear like that. As far as this poor man knew, the entire police force was corrupt, and now single-mindedly focused on keeping him close to their script, or else silencing him forever. That tape-recorded 911 call is what made Alex White heroic in my eyes.

White called the ATF again; some of their officers showed up at the BP station and took him back to their offices. They immediately contacted the Atlanta chief of police, who asked permission to send an Internal Affairs officer he trusted. They conducted a polygraph test on Alex White, a voice stress test, etc. Next, the officers of Internal Affairs had him call Arthur Tesler, J. R. Smith, Gregg Junnier, and Officer C. B. each in turn, to confirm the nature of the cover-up in which they were trying to involve him.

Later that night, Gregg Junnier called Alex White again and asked him where he was staying, so White now worried that Atlanta's Internal Affairs department was involved as well and had informed Gregg Junnier of the situation. That was when and why Alex White first contacted the Georgia Bureau of Investigations (GBI) and the Federal Bureau of Investigations (FBI).

On Thanksgiving Day, White talked to Officers Junnier and Smith again. They indicated that they had more money for him. J. R. Smith came to White's mother's home and seemed very upset. He confessed that his search warrant application was bogus and that in it he had falsely reported that Alex White had made a controlled buy for them at the Neal Street location. White pretended that he was still going along with the cover-up, for his own protection. J. R. Smith took Alex White to City Hall East, allegedly to do a police lineup when no one else was around. But in fact there was no lineup, just another $100 gift from J. R. Smith, along with a voucher he had White sign in order to cover the lying story about the original Neal Street buy. J. R. Smith next took him to the location of the alleged Neal Street buy; then the two men met Gregg Junnier at a store called Eddie's, where he received an additional $100 from Junnier. These random and repeated hundred dollar payments made everyone involved seem cheap, even Alex White.

But that same evening, Alex White called Fox 5 News. He appeared on television the very next day, and later that day the FBI requested an interview with him. This was the end of Alex White's cover—and a four-year career as a police informant (the fact that he had recently been arrested again on yet another drug charge suggested that he had been dropped and left to his own limited devices). After completing the television interview, Alex White met an FBI agent in a parking lot near City Hall East. The agent took him back to his mother's home, where he gathered his things and was taken to a hotel where he lived for the next six months. His life, White told us, had been upside-down ever since.

There was not much in this harrowing tale of police corruption for Mr. McKenney to contradict. All he cared about was distancing Arthur Tesler from the activities of all the other bad actors with whom Alex White had interacted. To that end, Mr. McKenney reiterated that Alex White originally came into contact with the Atlanta Narcotics Unit through Officer C. B., and that he worked mainly with Gregg Junnier and J. R. Smith, not Arthur Tesler. Officer Tesler had not been involved in any way in the exchange of money, the arrangement of transportation, or anything else. In fact, as Mr. McKenney underlined for us, Alex White never *saw* Arthur Tesler during the cover-up.

Nonetheless there had been phone calls, two of them at least. Since Alex White began keeping a very moving personal log of everything that happened in that chaotic and whirlwind week, he could tell us with great specificity about the phone calls. Both came on November 22, 2006—the day after the shooting—the first at 2:38 p.m. and the second at 3:03 p.m. Both calls lasted just under two minutes. Officer Tesler, White testified, was reiterating the details of the manufactured story about the controlled buy at Neal Street. It seemed a small connection, admittedly, but it was an important connection nonetheless.

After this essential and jarring testimony, we adjourned for the day.

~

For the next two days, we heard a battery of testimony, all of which was intended to corroborate the most shocking details of Alex White's story.

HH

HH, Alex White's mother, testified that he was indeed home all day on November 21, 2006, save for one half hour (5:00–5:30 p.m.) when he stepped out briefly. After he was taken away by the FBI on November 25, 2006, she did not see him again until Christmas.

II

II was the director of radio frequency in Georgia for Metro PCS. Since cell phone calls are normally bounced off of whatever radio tower is closest to the phone when it is being used, it is possible to trace the way in which a phone travels within a dense urban area like Atlanta. II confirmed that there was no electronic evidence that Alex White's phone ever moved out of the area where he was living with his mother on November 21, 2006. More to the point, II also confirmed that Alex White's cell phone was used to call Artur Tesler's phone on November 24, 2006, three days after the shooting.

JJ

JJ was the ATF Agent with whom Alex White worked, and who was involved in the initial investigation of the criminal search warrant and attendant cover-up. He corroborated Alex White's entire story, down to the details, but here once again, there was no mention of Arthur Tesler in those details.

KK

KK was a detective with the Atlanta Homicide Unit in 2006. He had been called in to investigate the 933 Neal Street address once it was redefined as a homicide crime scene. He could not speak to the cover-up, naturally, but he did confirm that Arthur Tesler never fired his weapon on the evening in question.

LL

LL was an investigator with the Atlanta Narcotics Unit Team 2. He was brought in to perform the posthumous search of Ms. Johnston's home. He testified that he received multiple phone calls from Arthur Tesler that evening, all of them inquiring as to whether any drugs had been found at 933 Neal Street. Officer LL also testified that he found the back basement door blocked with wooden beams but could not determine when they had been placed there.

MM

MM was an investigator with the Georgia Bureau of Investigation. He testified that, later that same evening, he found a stray bullet lodged in the ceiling of the porch at 933 Neal Street.

NN

NN was a firearms expert who testified that this bullet, removed from the ceiling at the Neal Street address, "probably" came from Kathryn Johnston's revolver, but that she could not be certain. She was also unable to determine decisively which guns had fired the bullets that had been recovered from Ms. Johnston's body during her autopsy.

XX

XX seemed the very picture of an FBI agent—tall and well built, extremely handsome in an aw-shucks, openhanded way, but also thoughtful, calm, and remarkably firm under Mr. Mckenney's intense cross-examination (this was the first and only time I saw Mr. McKenney as less than completely polite). He was immediately trustworthy and his testimony was compelling; it carried over from the afternoon of May 12 in to the following morning of May 13, 2008.

While Agent XX normally took notes on a legal pad when he conducted interviews, in Arthur Tesler's case—and damningly for him—there was a three-hour tape recording of the testimony that Officer Tesler gave to the FBI on December 7, 2006. We listened specifically to the portion in which Arthur Tesler lied about Alex White making a controlled buy at the

Neal Street address. Later, on December 21, 2006, Officer Tesler indicated to this same FBI agent that he wished to cooperate with the FBI's investigation, and to confess, but that he wanted to do so after the holidays, in order to inform his family of what had happened in November, and what was about to happen to him.

On January 4, 2007, Arthur Tesler had his meeting with Agent XX. He confirmed that he had lied about everything: the controlled buy; the conditions of the original search warrant; the details of J. R. Smith's briefing before the warrant was served; and the cover-up in which the three officers were engaged after Ms. Johnston's death.

Clearly, Arthur Tesler was guilty of the second charge the state had brought against him. He had indeed lied to the FBI; we had heard the tape.

9

The Human Cost

THE FINAL THREE WITNESSES the state called to conclude its case against Arthur Tesler turned our attention, quite properly, away from the police officers and other investigators who had worked on this case, and toward the victim herself. It seemed important to recall at least some of the details of the human life that had been lost in this tragic affair.

PP

If Agent XX was the epitome of the scholar-athlete turned FBI agent, then Dr. PP was the epitome of the filmic mortician, newly emerged from the dungeon of a state-run morgue. He was small and extremely thin, a rumpled man in a rumpled suit, but also earnest and remarkably thorough. It must be agonizing, this daily application of one's talents to studying the damage we humans do to one another. Offering his professional assessment on behalf of the Atlanta Forensics Unit, Dr. PP confirmed that Kathryn Johnston died of five or six gunshot wounds, and brought a generic sketch of the human body on which he had traced the trajectory of each of the bullets, including one that lodged near her heart and most likely was proximately responsible for her death. Due to the extent of her injuries, there would have been no way, and no time, in which to save her.

The sketch haunted me; it stood vertically on a table before the jury box while the doctor gave his testimony. When the first of Ms. Johnston's two neighbors was called to the stand, it was still there. We on the jury asked our own stalwart sergeant to take it down out of respect, and he, clearly mortified by this oversight, literally ran to do so.

RR

RR was an endearing elderly woman with weak eyesight, but there was something about the quiet dignity of her bearing that inspired the entire courtroom to defer to her. A near neighbor to Ms. Johnston, RR testified that she had been on the phone with Ms. Johnston for ten minutes, from approximately 6:06 p.m. to 6:16 p.m. She was thus the last person to speak to Kathryn Johnston alive; she hung up her phone less than fifteen minutes before Ms. Johnston was murdered.

SS

SS was an equally elegant middle-aged woman, impeccable in accoutrement and quieter in demeanor than her predecessor, RR, but every bit as gracious and polite. SS was another friend to Ms. Johnston, and she testified that she was on the phone with her for one half hour or more that same evening; in fact, the call lasted from 5:28 p.m. to 6:01 p.m.

Clearly the prosecutors had called these witnesses to confirm that no controlled buy had been attempted at 933 Neal Street at any time after it was first proposed around 5:00 p.m. But I was more taken with the life that this testimony described. A ninety-two-year-old woman, living alone, rounded out her day as winter darkness came on. She spent roughly forty-five minutes on the phone talking to friends, and indicated to the latter of them that she was going to bed as soon as they hung up.

Presumably Ms. Johnston did so, but before she could sleep she was roused from her room by the terrifying sound of people, unknown and unannounced, cutting through the burglar bars at her front door. She fished out an antique revolver that she seemed not to know how to use, fired errantly into her porch ceiling, and was felled in a hail of police gunfire. The numbers were also illuminating. Ms. Johnston had been shot five or six times, but the police had fired thirty-nine times. Less than 15 percent of the shots fired had reached their intended target, and more than three had certainly ricocheted, caroming off the doorway and striking fellow police officers already inside the premises. These officers could not have known who had shot them and must have feared they were being fired upon by people they could not see. Clearly, using a weapon in an active line of fire was a very different experience from doing so at a firing range, as these officers had all done earlier in the day. Given the false information they had received at J. R. Smith's briefing, these officers presumably believed that they had walked into an ambush and, confronted with an apparently well-armed enemy, began firing wildly inside the home of Ms. Johnston.

A more wrenching end to her life was unimaginable to me. The state prosecutors rested their case at noon, and we adjourned for the day.

~

As this book was going to press, I had the privilege of meeting with the Reverend Anthony W. Motley of the Lindsey Street Baptist Church in Atlanta. An alumnus of the Ohio State University, Morehouse College, and the Interdenominational Theological Center (ITC) in Atlanta, Reverend Motley has long been one of the most eloquent—and assuredly the most prophetic—of the several ecclesiastical voices that have been raised in understandable outrage at the damage that was done to the fabric of the local community by the killing of Ms. Johnston. Reverend Motley was one of the only pastors who attended the impromptu gathering at Ms. Johnston's home when it was still an active crime scene, on the very same night she was killed. He later lent the Lindsey Street facilities to those members of the community who were grappling with their anger and sense of moral outrage, struggling to come to terms with what had happened there, and attempting to imagine what new kinds of institutional oversight and community liaisons might work to prevent such tragedies in the future. His church provided a forum in which voice was given to anger, but choreographed in such a way as to be formed and channeled into moral cadences that avoided the descent into blind rage.[1] But for the airing of such powerful grievances in such a public setting, the community in and around Neal Street might well have exploded in such rage.

Unlike most public figures who became deeply involved in Ms. Johnston's cause at the outset, Reverend Motley has never stopped talking about her. He worries, as I do, that the payment of a cash settlement to her family may invite the false conclusion that the case is now closed. The profound issues this case raised (and still raises) clearly demonstrate that such a case

1. For more on the relationship between the expression of justified anger, tempered by the relevant virtues, as essential for the avoidance of blind rage or despair, see Jeffrey Stout, *Blessed Are the Organized*, 53–69. As he puts it later in the book: "The ethical transformation of citizens includes the transformation of grief and rage into tempered anger and courageous practical wisdom" (227).

will never, and should never, be closed. "Closure" is not a relevant category in such matters. Continual community vigilance is the key. To that end, Reverend Motley has also been deeply involved in the Atlanta Citizen's Review Board (ACRB) that was established in 2007 in the wake of this tragedy,[2] and he insists on keeping Ms. Johnston's memory alive both in his own community and in the city's collective conscience—from the mayor's office to the streets and parks nearer to her home.

Reverend Motley spoke passionately of the need for some more concrete way to memorialize Ms. Johnston and what the taking of her life meant to the local community in particular. She is, he candidly observes, central to this community's identity now, whether the community wishes it or not. Indeed, he went so far as to suggest that her death had done for this community what Jesus' death did for the local Jewish community in Jerusalem two thousand years ago. I was shaken awake by that almost casual observation and have mulled it over many times since our initial conversation.

What might it mean to view Kathryn Johnston as a Christ figure? It might seem that there is abundant Christian precedent for such a view: many of the early martyrs were conceived in Christ-comparative ways. Theirs was seen as an *enactment*, the imitation of Christ's passion and death. But the comparison hinges on a great deal more than the apparent fact that both Jesus and Ms. Johnston died due to what we now know to have been an unjust exercise of police power, one in which many of the normal institutions of community oversight—not to say of mercy—failed rather dramatically.

Instead, the essential connection between Christ's death and Ms. Johnston's will be the way in which a community chooses to commemorate it. As my dear friend Richard Carp of St. Mary's College of California has observed, the most profound question Jesus' disciples faced most likely came one year after his death: How should they celebrate the Passover *this* year? Should they return to Jerusalem? Should they do again what they had done with him the previous year? Should they add a more explicit commemoration of the loss of their leader to the traditional rituals they already knew by heart? Clearly, at some point, the emerging Christian community made the commemoration of Christ's death at Easter the centerpiece of their new ritual calendar, replacing the older Passover liturgy their Jewish fellows continued to uphold. The community, in short, was becoming a community of memory, a community committed to recalling, each and

2. See the review board's Web site: http://acrbgov.org/.

every year, a violence that had been done, in order to be reminded anew of what those shattering events meant to a living community now.

Reverend Motley articulated in almost lyrical terms the need he believes our community has for such ritual commemoration, where Ms. Johnston is concerned. Why, he wonders, do we not gather at 933 Neal Street each year—police and civilians, rich and poor, black and white—to commemorate what was done there, in order to rededicate ourselves to the sacred task of working for social justice? I include Arthur Tesler in that somber invitation; he has now been released from prison, and has completed his penitentiary service. It will be as important to fold him back into the community as it is to weave Ms. Johnston's memory into the tapestry of Atlanta's public life.

It is ironic, Reverend Motley added, that we know so very little about Ms. Johnston's life; her family has been noticeably (and understandably) reticent to talk publicly about her. I was reminded as I listened to the pastor develop these Christian connections that we know very little about the so-called historical Jesus as well. What we have in the gospels is not biography so much as it is a community's commemoration of the meaning they continued to find in the manner, and the making, of his death—as well as the new sacred institutions that emerged in the wake of the community's attempt to grapple with the original tragedy.[3] Reverend Motley's moral challenge to his own community is that it engage in similar acts of pious regard and collective commemoration. What finer purpose could be served by the cash award the family has received from the city, he asks, than a memorial to this woman and a public testament to this tragic circuit of events? A public park, a public library, a community institution dedicated in her name, committed to and structured around such sacred remembering, perhaps with an annual ritual of remembrance on the 21st of November, before the national Thanksgiving holiday: that is what Reverend Motley feels is most urgently needed today.

A trial by jury could not provide that, nor could a cash award, as I see more clearly only now.

---

3. I develop some of the themes of a Gethsemane-centered Christianity in *Tragic Posture and Tragic Vision: Against the Modern Failure of Nerve* (New York: Continuum, 1994), 181–29, and focus more explicitly on the dynamics of gospel-creation in *This Tragic Gospel: How John Corrupted the Heart of Christianity* (San Francisco: Jossey-Bass, 2008).

See finally my short essay "Good Friday Christianity," *The Huffington Post* (April 6, 2012). Online: http://www.huffingtonpost.com/louis-a-ruprecht-jr/good-friday-christianity_b_1403279.html.

10

Defending the Indefensible

THE CASE THAT MR. McKenney offered in defense of Arthur Tesler was brief and lasted a single day, May 14, 2008. Everything hinged on Tesler himself, whom we had witnessed sitting rather passively and emotionless at the defense table throughout this trial. His time had finally come. Almost as a way to deflate the intensity of that situation, and to take the singular focus off of Officer Tesler, Mr. McKenney called another police officer to the stand first.

TT

This was TT, a member of Atlanta's RED DOG Canine Narcotics Unit we had previously heard about. He had graduated from the police academy in June 2000 with Arthur Tesler; they had remained close friends since then, and they obviously worked together quite often.

For some reason, Officer TT was also at the briefing before the raid on Neal Street; presumably the narcotics team was preparing to search the house for drugs after securing the scene with their search warrant. Tragically, when this scene almost immediately became a homicide crime scene, it would be many hours before Officer TT's colleague, EE, was finally permitted to investigate the Neal Street address at around 2:00 a.m.

Officer TT testified that he did not hear J. R. Smith say anything about a controlled buy during the briefing, but he admitted that he did not remember many details from the briefing and was not paying close attention, since the details of the search warrant, or the raid, did not directly concern him. He would not be storming the house; his job was simply to search it with his dog once the place was secured.

This seemed a minor detail, but it was interesting. Mr. McKenney was trying to establish reasonable doubt in our minds by suggesting that it was just possible that Arthur Tesler never knew about the lie(s) that enabled J. R. Smith to receive the search warrant in the first place. Tesler was not inside the Fulton County jail when Officer Smith made the original application. He might never have read the relevant details of the search warrant in the car on the way to the briefing (though Gregg Junnier testified that he did). And now the implication was that Arthur Tesler never heard J. R. Smith mention the lie—the one about Alex White making a controlled buy at 933 Neal Street—at the briefing before they moved en masse to Neal Street. All of this, Mr. McKenney was suggesting, came out after the fact, and after Ms. Johnston's tragic demise.

To make good on that increasingly implausible suggestion, we would need to hear from the man himself.

Arthur Tesler

We had seen many striking personalities, and many memorable faces, in the course of this trial: the colossal biceps of an officer from the Narcotics Canine Unit; the quiet elegance of one of Arthur Tesler's teammates, the agonized and tearful recollections of another; the mortuary macabre of a forensic pathologist; the hoodlum affect of a down-and-out drug dealer; the long-suffering dignity of Ms. Johnston's neighbors and friends.

In contrast to all of this, Arthur Tesler seemed almost featureless to me. He was of medium height and slightly overweight, with a wide face, short hair, unimaginative eyes, and a surprisingly soft voice. He was trying very hard to be polite and likeable. Perhaps that was what had gotten him into trouble in the first place—the simple desire to be liked and accepted by his peers I thought. I know it cannot be as simple as that.

Arthur Tesler was on the witness stand all day, until we concluded at about 5:30 p.m. It must have been exhausting for him.[1] I simply could not muster sympathy for the man I had heard about who did what he did in November 2006; I reserved that for Kathryn Johnston. But this man grieved me in May 2008. I am put to wonder what kind of character he possesses now, in 2013.

---

1. Tesler's testimony—consisting of Direct Examination, Cross-Examination, Re-Direct Examination, Re-Cross Examination and a second re-Direct Examination—takes up most of Volume XIV of the trial transcripts, pages 24–295.

For all of the swirl of detail covered in his long testimony, the essence of the case boiled down to two simple facts, and the question of how Arthur Tesler was related to them both. First, J. R. Smith lied about making a controlled buy in order to secure the original search warrant. If Arthur Tesler knew about this before they served the search warrant and before the killing of Ms. Johnston, then he was culpable. Second, J. R. Smith and Gregg Junnier organized a cover-up immediately after the death of Ms. Johnston, beginning that very night at the crime scene. If Arthur Tesler assisted them with that cover-up, including lying to the FBI, until he had a crisis of conscience and a change of heart, then he was guilty of that charge as well.

His denials were predictable. He never beat Fabian Sheats. He was busy doing the paperwork for Sheats's arrest when his colleagues began concocting what proved to be a disastrous plan. He was not paying attention when J. R. Smith went into the jail to get the warrant. He was not paying attention to the details of the conditions for the search warrant, and in any case he never read it. Then came a small detail, designed to make him seem sympathetic, but instead it raised new questions for me. Tesler, like many of his colleagues, worked other jobs to supplement his limited income (most often, these officers tended to work as security guards). Arthur Tesler was also very involved in charity work. He was supposed to attend a charity ball with his wife that evening. She called him to finalize plans just when J. R. Smith began his briefing. Phone records suggested that he was on the phone for less than two minutes. Arthur Tesler claimed that J. R. Smith's briefing lasted little more than that. So Mr. McKenney's contention appeared to be twofold: first, that J. R. Smith did not mention the lies he had used to get the search warrant at the briefing; and second, that Arthur Tesler did not hear his colleague's briefing. I suppose this was designed to compound our doubts, but it seemed a little forced to me: "nothing unusual or incriminating was said at a briefing I did not hear."

When they got to the house on Neal Street, Officer Tesler told us that he was stationed at the rear of the house by the basement door. His job was to contain the perimeter and to detain anyone who tried to run away. No one ever did, naturally. Instead, he heard a barrage of gunfire at the front of the house, but was not permitted to leave his position until he was relieved later by other officers. When he finally got to the front of the house, Ms. Johnston was dead and his colleagues were being prepared for transport to Grady Hospital. He simply had not done anything at 933 Neal Street.

It appeared to me that Arthur Tesler was trying to have it both ways. He admitted that he knew Officers Smith and Junnier were rogue police officers, but that he did not know this particular search warrant was suspicious. So much for the killing of Ms. Johnston.

The matter of the cover-up came next, and in this case, there were a number of relevant details that he simply could not shake. His motivations notwithstanding, Arthur Tesler lied and falsified police reports on November 21st and 22nd, 2006. He destroyed evidence on November 22, 2006 (this involved the rest of the found drugs that J. R. Smith had used to plant evidence at the Neal Street address after the shooting; Tesler admitted that, under coercion, he helped J. R. Smith throw the remaining drugs into a storm drain—he believed that if he did not do so, then Officer J. R. Smith would attempt to frame him). He lied to the FBI on December 7, 2006. Two weeks later, on December 21, 2006, when the FBI already knew that he had been lying to them, Arthur Tesler agreed to cooperate with their investigation. And so on January 4, 2007, he signed the proffer agreement that required him never to veer from the story that incriminated him again.

FBI Agent J. R. was very clear and concise in laying out what Arthur Tesler knew and when he knew it. In this agent's opinion, Arthur Tesler "knew" that the search warrant was bad, participated fully in J. R. Smith's briefing, did nothing wrong at the raid, but participated fully in the cover-up. Excepting that first point about the search warrant, we heard nothing in a full day of testimony from Tesler himself to contradict that sad story. It seemed to me that Mr. McKenney had performed admirably, making the most of a terrible situation and a terrible case. His suggestion was that we already had the two men who were directly responsible for Ms. Johnston's death in custody, and that the prosecutors were being excessive now in going after a new guy who was pressured into helping his superiors with a cover-up. If he could make Arthur Tesler seem sympathetic, then that story had some legs.

Ms. Hill had a rather subtle, and even brilliant, way of handling that, it seemed to me. Recalling the dramatic final exchange with Gregg Junnier, she put the same questions to Arthur Tesler:

> Q: Did you need training from the Atlanta Police Department to know the difference between the truth and a lie?
>
> A: No. . . .
>
> Q: Did you need training from the Atlanta Police Department to know the difference between right and wrong?
>
> A: No.[2]

2. Trial transcripts, Volume XIV, page 152.

When Gregg Junnier was asked the same questions, he suggested that you *did* need training to know right from wrong. He was essentially confessing the dirty secret of narcotics policing in Atlanta at the time—namely, that everyone got *trained* into a certain kind of policing, and everyone learned the corners you could get away with cutting. Violating certain citizens' rights was a part of the job; you simply had to trust your ability to make that assessment, and to decide when and where to do so. Playing fast and loose with the rules was fine when you were dealing with a Fabian Sheats; the tragedy came when Ms. Johnston's rights were violated.

Gregg Junnier had been very forthright in his self-description: he had ceased to be a virtuous person on the job; he had learned a rather distorted way of distinguishing right from wrong. And the human cost of his viciousness would clearly haunt him for the rest of his days.

By contrast, Arthur Tesler was still clinging to the image he had of himself as a good person, a virtuous person with real moral clarity. But his answer—that you do *not* need training to know right from wrong—ironically took away his right to say that he was not wrong to lie to the homicide investigators, and later to the FBI.

The story that had emerged was, for me, painful in its simplicity and comprehensibility. Arthur Tesler, by his own repeated admission, was not paying attention; he was a pleaser, slightly weak-willed, neither virtuous nor vicious but placid and unresisting. He wanted to be liked, and he was willing to go along with what others told him to do. The absence of the relevant virtues—like moral courage and a heightened sense of justice—in such a setting can be deadly. In a funny way, then, the best thing that could have happened to Arthur Tesler was this: to be caught and punished for doing something comparatively minor, like lying, before getting caught for doing something much worse. There was no doubt in my mind about that last point: if Arthur Tesler was not yet "dirty," he was being *trained* to be. He had chosen the two men to whom he wished to be apprenticed. In a couple of years more, he would have been just like them.

Based solely on FBI Agent J. R.'s testimony, Officer Tesler's grueling day on the stand, supplemented by testimony from Gregg Junnier and Alex White, Arthur Tesler seemed guilty of something. Naming that something would prove to be a complicated matter, however.

11

Deliberation and Judgment

THE CLOSING ARGUMENT MADE by the prosecutors was fairly simple. We knew what they were alleging, and we had learned the nuances of the story as they saw it over the long course of three weeks of testimony. We were being asked to consider three separate charges:

1. that Arthur Tesler violated his Oath of Office on the evening of November 21, 2006, when Kathryn Johnston was killed;

2. that Arthur Tesler made false statements to the FBI regarding an alleged controlled buy he had witnessed earlier that same day, prior to the application for the fatal no-knock warrant that resulted in Ms. Johnston's death;

3. that Arthur Tesler falsely imprisoned Ms. Johnston by guarding the back door of the house when the rest of his narcotics team stormed the front door and killed Ms. Johnston.

The first two of those charges seemed well beyond reasonable questioning, I thought, but the third one seemed like a case of prosecutorial overreaching, a minor version of the same thing in which Tesler and his colleagues were accused of being involved. The horrible series of events that seemed to unfold in slow motion, leading inexorably to Ms. Johnston's death on the 21st of November 2006, all involved behaviors that were utterly incompatible with sound policing according to any reasonable definition of honor and appropriate conduct. Citizens' rights had been trampled, serially violated day after day, and it stretched credulity to ask us to believe that Arthur Tesler did not know that. As he himself had admitted, you don't need special training to know right from wrong. The wrongs in this case were overwhelming—and fatal.

As to the second charge, we had heard with our own ears Arthur Tesler lying to FBI agents during his first recorded interview.

As to the third charge, it seemed that the prosecutors felt that Officer Tesler's position at the back door of 933 Neal Street, with the implicit duty to "contain and detain," was the equivalent of falsely imprisoning Ms. Johnston in her home, since the original search warrant was falsified. I understood how they viewed the matter, but I could not think my way to their conclusion; no one ever got near that basement door, and with it boarded up (as it appeared to have been), no one ever would have. (The only ones who apparently spent time in the basement were J. R. Smith, when he planted drugs there, and the canine unit officer who later found the drugs there.) True, Arthur Tesler had no business being at that address that evening, and yet ironically, 933 Neal Street was the one place where he did not seem to me to have done anything wrong that day.[1]

Mr. McKenney surprised me by arguing forcefully, and well, against all three charges. His reasoning concerning the third charge was very much in line with my own thinking. But his argument about the Oath of Office brought the surprise. He called our attention to the precise *wording* of the charge the prosecutors had brought against his client. We were being asked to assess whether Arthur Tesler had violated his Oath of Office, not in general terms, but specifically at Ms. Johnston's home on the night she was killed. Upon reflection, that did seem a harder argument to make, unless one assumed, as I did, that Officer Tesler had no business being at that address at all that day, and that they were a series of dishonorable actions earlier in the day that violated the essence of his oath "to protect and to serve" the people.

Mr. McKenney's argument against the second charge was passed over fairly quickly, and seemed to involve a technicality about who had proper

---

1. As I have suggested, and viewed in hindsight years later, I note that the precise wording of the Georgia statute that Officer Tesler was accused of violating lends credence to the prosecutors' view of the matter. It reads as follows: "*Official Code of Georgia 16–15-42. False imprisonment under color of legal process.* When the arrest, confinement, or detention of a person by warrant, mandate, or process is manifestly illegal and shows malice and oppression, an officer issuing or knowingly and maliciously executing the same shall, upon conviction thereof, be removed from office and punished by imprisonment for not less than one nor more than ten years."

It does seem accurate to say that Officer Tesler "knowingly and maliciously execut[ed]" a bogus search warrant that evening; it is noteworthy that the maximum penalty for this crime (ten years) was twice that to which he would have been subject for the other two.

jurisdiction if Arthur Tesler was not in Fulton County when he lied to the FBI. For all of his intelligence, and what had truly been a bravura performance throughout the trial, even Mr. McKenney seemed uncomfortable with this argument (I was quite wrong about that, since our jury's conviction of Officer Tesler on the second count of the indictment was overturned by a superior court for this very reason). It appeared to me that Mr. McKenney hoped that, by walking us very clearly and emphatically through the obvious holes in the logic of the third charge, and the imprecision in the language of the first, then he would lead us to the way of thinking that would incline us to give his client a pass. His was a heroic performance against long odds, from the first day to the last.

As I was processing all of this information, the presiding judge gave us our final instructions as to the law, our responsibilities in deliberating, and so on. After having been prohibited from talking with my fellow jurors about the case, I was eager to be about our business. I had grown fond of them all, and we had grown into a caring community, one whose members had come to share a solidarity born of long and difficult experience. We had learned one another's dietary needs, restrictions, and preferences, had taken turns bringing coffee and tea and treats to the jury room each morning, and had begun to welcome each other, albeit tentatively, into small details from our personal lives. It had been a long forced march, and now at last we could rest in the shade of the trees and talk together.

Without knowing the specifics of how individuals felt, I had a pretty clear idea of how some of my fellow jurors would be leaning. Some were clearly mindful of the sacred principle of being innocent until *proven* guilty, and that it was our sacred duty to insist on the proof. Others coupled that concern with razor-sharp intelligence and close attention to precision and to the meaning of words. Some of those persons might well be disinclined to find Officer Tesler guilty on the first and third counts. Others were so clearly outraged by the death of Ms. Johnston—and their rage was mingled with great grief—that the strong temptation would be to throw the book at him, finding him guilty on all three counts. As I have indicated, my initial impression was that he was guilty of the first two counts against him, but probably innocent of the third. I was eager to hear how my fellow jurors saw the facts of this case, and how they were thinking their way to their own conclusions.

But it was not to be. As soon as we gathered in the jury room, our stalwart sergeant called out three names, mine included. We three (two white men and one white woman) had been alternate jurors all along, he informed us, and would not be a part of this jury's deliberations. We were taken immediately to a small room adjacent to the courtroom, where we had what seemed to me the most unenviable job of all: *empty, purposeless waiting.* The jury's deliberations began on Thursday, May 15th, went on for four days and spanned a weekend, until a verdict was finally announced on the afternoon of Tuesday, May 20th.

We were called back into the courtroom several times during the jury's deliberations. Once the jury, in the person of the foreman, asked to have a transcript of Officer Tesler's testimony read back to them. Once the jury reconvened to pose a procedural question to the judge. My fellow jurors looked very tired, with nerves stretched very thin. When we gathered in the jury room each evening to adjourn for the day, things had clearly reached the point where they were finding it difficult to talk further. Several of my fellow jurors had obviously been crying; others were tight-lipped and frustrated. All seemed exhausted. It was heartbreaking to see; I cared deeply for these people, all of them, and sympathized with their thankless task.

The three of us who were alternates could only speculate as to how they were deliberating, and what ways various persons were leaning. We were uncertain whether we were permitted to discuss the case among ourselves, so we touched on the details of the trial, but really only in passing. We talked more about our fellow jurors and wondered how they were holding up; we also talked, a lot, about our plans for after the trial concluded.[2]

2. So concerned had I become at the emotional state of our jury that I typed a short letter to the presiding judge on Friday, the second full day of the jury's deliberations.

> 16 May 2008
> Dear Judge Johnson:
>
> I am uncertain if I, as alternative juror, am permitted to pose questions to and through our foreperson, but if so, and in light of yesterday's question from the jury and your response to it, I would ask for clarification of the following question: Is this a fair representation of the "division of labor'" in a jury trial:
> The attorneys present the evidence to the jury.
> The judge presents the charges and explains the relevant law to the jury.
> The jury decides how *any of* the evidence relates to *each of* the charges.
> Once again: is this a fair and accurate reflection of our role and duties at this point?
> If this is permissible, may I ask you to pass this question on to the foreperson?
> My thanks to you for your kindness and professionalism throughout this proceeding.
> Sincerely yours,
> Louis A. Ruprecht Jr.

My purpose in framing the question in this way was to underline what seemed in danger of being lost in a sea of details and lingering doubts about such details. We on the jury were the sole *interpreters* of what had happened, as well as of how the law related

~

Eventually our jury found its way to a consensus. They found Arthur Tesler guilty on the second of the three charges; Officer Tesler gasped and openly wept when he heard the result. We immediately reconvened in the jury room, and everyone was very emotional. We were torn between a desire to spring from that room and never return, and the desire to linger, to remain close to one another, and to acknowledge the gravity and the intensity of what we'd been through. The prosecutors, Ms. Hill and Mr. Odum, came back to the jury room to thank us and to talk briefly about what we had felt, doubted, or believed, and how we had come to our conclusions. Peter Odum, who had been so restrained and quietly firm, now smiled broadly, doubtless relieved that the thing was over. Kellie Hill made a point of telling me that she regretted that I was an alternate juror, since she had assessed from my demeanor that I was leaning her way. I was, for the most part. I had grown to like her, too. I had grown to like and admire everyone involved—all three attorneys, the judge, and fourteen of my fellow citizen jurors. We had, all of us, done very good work, a work of terrifying responsibility.

The sentencing hearing was scheduled two days later on Thursday, May 22, and Judge Johnson invited any jurors who wished to attend to do so. He cautioned us to arrive early, as there was sure to be a crowd. He was correct.

~

Three of us returned for the sentencing hearing. It felt odd to be back in the courtroom after a day away, strange to go through the security screening downstairs with a new crop of jurors, many of whose juridical adventures were just beginning. The courtroom was packed to standing room capacity; television cameras lined the back of the courtroom. When the court officers

---

to what had happened. We were not beholden to anyone, just to the evidence and the relevant laws. I was also trying, in the third line about *any* evidence and *each* charge, to underline the importance of disentangling the three charges; if the jury was hung up on one of the charges (and my guess was that it was indeed split on the first), then this need not create confusion about the clearest of the charges, the second.

While this was unknown to me, Judge Johnson did discuss my letter and the possibility of raising its questions with the Jury on May 5, 2008. The letter was entered into evidence as C-7. Judge Johnson's view was that "the more you talk to jurors about the charges, the more confused they become, quite frankly. And the more the Court tries to explain the questions or answer the questions that they have, the more dangerous—or we become dangerously close to confusing the jurors and possibly heading towards a mistrial" [Volume XVI of the trial transcripts, pages 4–5]. I was gratified to read that my letter at least "gave [Judge Johnson] some idea of how the jurors are thinking about the explanation that I gave to them yesterday."

saw us, they invited us to take our old seats in the jury box; I was seated
two seats away from the Reverend Al Sharpton. This time, Arthur Tesler
was not dressed in a suit; he was no longer a free man. He was brought
into the courtroom in a prison jumpsuit and handcuffs. It was a shocking
indication of the power of the judgment we had held in our hands all along.
In that moment, Arthur Tesler became a sympathetic fellow sufferer, to me
another brother in the same distress.

We heard some testimony that spoke to the aggravating and mitigating
circumstances that would counsel for or against leniency in the sentencing
of Mr. Tesler. Perhaps the most telling evidence was presented by Atlanta
Chief of Police Richard Pennington, who informed us of the social cost of
this scandal. The Atlanta Narcotics Unit, which had already been gutted
financially and reduced from five teams to two, was completely disbanded
after the revelation of the events that led to Ms. Johnston's death. For over
one year, there was no targeted narcotics policing anywhere in the city. The
dealers knew this, and a large piece of the distribution infrastructure moved
to Atlanta from further south in Miami. In addition, most of the cases in
which these three officers had been involved would have to be dismissed.
Chief Pennington believed that it would take many years to undo the damage that had been done in the vacuum created by this case.

Arthur Tesler's wife testified to his qualities as a father, a husband, a
family man, and a volunteer in his community. I had no doubt that all of
this was true. That was a part of the tragedy of the thing. He was not a bad
man, but he was not a virtuous man either. Arthur Tesler was a decidedly
mixed bag, which is why I thought of Shakespeare at the time, and still do:

> For no thought is contented. The better sort,
> As thoughts of things divine, are intermix'd
> With scruples, and do set the word itself
> Against the word . . .

He was "intermix'd," set tragically against himself and his better self. He
was not evil; like every tragic character, he had not sinned, he had simply
missed it somehow. Arthur Tesler had made choices that had started him
down a road of increasing lawlessness, ruthlessness, and viciousness. If this
conviction stopped his downward slide, then good might yet come of this.
But at a horrific cost to many.

The judge retired to his chambers—but not for long. He sentenced
Arthur Tesler to the maximum of five years imprisonment and expressed his
personal dismay at the behaviors that had been revealed during the trial. He

was thoughtful, but he was outraged too. He very graciously called us, the three jurors in attendance, back into his chambers, and we visited with him for nearly an hour. He was relaxed, eloquent, sure of himself and of his judgments. He confessed to us his own view on all three counts, but also expressed a very moving commitment to, and trust in, the democratic jury system. It had been his experience that, when twelve reasonable citizens deliberate in good faith with one another, then the consensus view they can all agree to is usually the correct one. He thanked us for being those citizens. It was a fitting final exchange to have in a courthouse I gratefully left for the last time.[3]

3. The Honorable Michael D. Johnson retired from the Fulton County bench in order to run as a Democrat for the 5th Congressional District of Georgia. He declared his candidacy on May 23, 2012, seeking to unseat the long-time Congressman and Civil Rights activist John Lewis. Running in response to the Congress's unprecedented low approval rating, and out of his conviction that long-term congressional representatives he referred to as "the decades club," including Lewis, had shown themselves unable or unwilling to work in a bipartisan way to secure significant legislative results, Johnson was nonetheless soundly defeated in the Democratic primary election on July 31, 2012 (he received 19 percent of the vote compared to Lewis's 81 percent). Lewis easily retained his congressional seat in the general election on November 6, 2012.

Epilogue

Born wrong. Could be as simple as that. Wrong parents. Wrong country. Or
born anywhere, eminently decent, but on the wrong side of a bad law. Then
there's the luck that separates forgotten incident from criminal one . . . I think
too of the children I might have killed had they timed their carelessness just
right, a trace of liquor on my breath, their ball rolling into the street, my car
going slightly faster than slow. Fingerprinted. Front-paged. Instead, a normal
evening at home, a citizen, nearly upright. Aren't most of us, caught or not,·
responsible for some kind of choice?

STEPHEN DUNN, "CRIMINAL," IN *RIFFS & RECIPROCITIES* (1998)

~

THERE ARE MANY WAYS in which to view the events that I have described in
this book; I myself am deeply ambivalent about many of them. Ultimately
this was not a simple story with good guys and bad guys, not to my eye
(though we met plenty of both). It was a very human story in which I too,
as a democratic citizen, was deeply implicated. To be sure, there were staggering systemic failures that enabled these two (or three, or more) police
officers to game the system as they did. But those same officers were under
enormous pressure themselves: the pressure of being underpaid and overworked; the pressure to cover an ever-widening beat in the current regime
of severe budget cuts for all state-funded services, policing included; the
pressure to manufacture arrests, to apply for and serve increasing numbers
of search warrants. These pressures are intensified in a social environment,
and a cultural moment, in which we have grown comfortable with the notion that we need to proceed as if we were waging *a war* against drugs—or

to put it more precisely, a war against those who manufacture and distribute and (occasionally) consume drugs. The tragic result was the loss of an innocent human life, agonizing collateral damage in that war.

Viewed one way, the accountability structures we have in place worked rather well, albeit after the fact. The kind of rogue policing to which we were introduced did indeed generate immediate press interest and public outcry. Further investigation by the Atlanta Police Department and the FBI, and the activity of several people most directly involved in the cover-up, sometimes outrageous and sometimes heroic, led to revelations of serial misconduct that resulted in multiple arrests and dismissals. We on the jury served our role as final arbiters of such oversight in rendering the verdict that quite properly (in my view) named Arthur Tesler's involvement as criminal.

The city of Atlanta's decision to award Ms. Johnston's family $4.9 million in recompense, while very dramatic, is hardly the end of this story. The structural problems that enabled these events to unfold as they did have not yet been sufficiently addressed, and symbolic actions—such as the very public and televised sentencing of Officer Tesler, or the enormous financial award to Ms. Johnston's family—are insufficient.

Viewed another way, we and the system both may have failed. Several months after the fact, Arthur Tesler's verdict was overturned on January 15, 2009, by the Georgia Appeals Court.[1] The reasoning behind their decision to overturn the ruling of our jury may seem maddeningly technical, but as I learned, the law *is* technical, and careful democratic deliberation can be very wordy and very difficult. It proved significant that Arthur Tesler was found guilty of only one of the three charges that the State of Georgia had brought against him, and acquitted of the other two. In his closing argument, Mr. McKenney had only casually mentioned that curious question of "venue"; apparently, he did so most effectively.

To explain how he did so, it is important to recall the precise wording of the Georgia law that Arthur Tesler was found guilty of violating:

> *Official Code of Georgia* 16–10–20. *False statements and writings, concealment of facts, and fraudulent documents in matters within jurisdiction of state or political subdivisions.*
> A person who knowingly and willfully falsifies, conceals, or covers up by any trick, scheme, or device a material fact; makes a false, fictitious, or fraudulent statement or representation; or makes or uses any false writing or document, knowing the same to contain

1. *Tesler v. State*, 295, *Georgia Appeals Reports* 569 (2009).

any false, fictitious, or fraudulent statement or entry, in any matter within the jurisdiction of any department or agency of state
government or of the government of any county, city, or other
political subdivision of this state shall, upon conviction thereof, be
punished by a fine of not more than $1,000.00 or by imprisonment
for not less than one nor more than five years, or both.

The Georgia Appeals Court analyzed the meaning of that law in the following way:

Under OCGA § 16–10–20, a person may commit the crime of
giving a false statement in one of three ways: (1) by using "any
trick, scheme, or device" to falsify or conceal a material fact; (2)
by affirmatively making a false statement or representation; or
(3) by knowingly making or using a false writing. . . . The indictment, however, specifically charged Tesler with violating OCGA §
16–10–20 by using a scheme (the agreement to cover up Smith's
falsification of the warrant application) to conceal or falsify a
material fact. Thus, the criminal conduct charged occurred at the
time and place where Tesler actually lied to investigators—i.e., at
the offices of the FBI.

The wording of the original law might suggest that this whole thing hinged
on a technicality concerning "jurisdiction," and up to a point it did. Arthur
Tesler lied to a *federal* agent, not to state or local police. But the majority
of justices on the Georgia Appeals Court was very clear that this was not
the problem (one dissenting justice disagreed). The majority reasoned that
state and local investigators were working with the FBI in this case so they
did have jurisdiction. However, the issue hinged on an even more madden-
ing detail. The one fact that was never presented in the trial was the precise
location of the FBI office in which Agent J. R. taped Arthur Tesler's lying
testimony on December 7, 2006. All the State of Georgia needed to do was
to present evidence that these offices were in fact located in Fulton County,
which would confirm that the court that tried him (a Fulton County Superior Court) had the proper jurisdiction to do so. The majority-minus-one
on the appeals court suggested in conclusion that Arthur Tesler could be
retried, if such evidence were available, and concluded with what sounded
like real sympathy for the reasoning of our jury: "In conclusion, we reverse
Tesler's conviction but hold that the evidence supported the jury's finding
that Tesler's conduct violated OCGA § 16–10–20. Should the State be able
to prove venue, therefore, it may retry Tesler on Count 2 of the indictment."[2]

2. In a cautionary footnote, the majority also noted that the jury had been improperly

There was no second trial, mercifully enough. By then, Arthur Tesler had also been indicted on federal charges of conspiring to violate civil rights, resulting in death. He pled guilty to that crime on October 30, 2008, with the understanding that U.S. Attorneys would recommend a relatively long sentence in federal prison. All three Atlanta narcotics investigators implicated in this case were sentenced on February 24, 2009: J. R. Smith received a ten-year term in federal prison, Gregg Junnier received a six-year term, and Arthur Tesler received a five-year term; each term was to be served without the possibility of parole. The three men were also required to issue a collective payment of $8,180.00 for the funeral expenses of Ms. Johnston, and each man will be supervised for three years upon his respective release from federal prison.[3]

The temptation, of course, is to end the story here, to put a man in jail and then all too conveniently to forget about him. That is how most courtroom dramas end, with the evildoer swept away in handcuffs, justice served. While we are very adept at putting people away for very long periods of time—as a people, we can seem almost eager to do so, since incarceration has become a booming business[4]—we do a very poor job of deliberating about their reintegration into our society after they have served their time and paid their punitive debt to society. We have, wittingly or no, created a strange class of person—the criminal inmate—whom we tend not to imagine any longer

instructed by the judge: "In light of the possibility that the State may retry Tesler, we note that the trial court erroneously instructed the jury that it could find Tesler guilty of violating OCGA § 16-10-20 if it found that he made a false statement using any one of the three methods set forth in the statute."

In other words, the wording of the indictment suggested that Mr. Tesler could only be found guilty of using a scheme when he lied to the FBI, and that only if it could be proven that the lie was spoken in an office located in Fulton County.

3. See http://www.justice.gov/opa/pr/2009/February/09-crt-159.html.

4. One of this system's most eloquent critics—since she was a victim of its excess and overreach—is Angela Y. Davis, now a professor at the University of California, Santa Cruz. Her important works include *Angela Davis—An Autobiography* (New York: Random House, 1974), *Are Prisons Obsolete?* (New York: Seven Stories, 2003), and *The Meaning of Freedom and Other Difficult Dialogues* (San Francisco: City Lights, 2012). I am indebted to my friend and colleague James Winchester for these references.

Another striking description of this social and moral terrain comes from Mike Davis in an exposé entitled "Hell Factories in the Field: A Prison-Industrial Complex," *The Nation* 260.7 (February 20, 1995) 229–33. Davis developed this theme in *Ecology of Fear: Los Angeles and the Imagination of Disaster* (New York: Henry Holt, 1998) 411–18. The story of the privatization of such military and prison industrial (and now for profit) complexes is well described in Naomi Klein, *The Shock Doctrine: The Rise of Disaster Capitalism* (New York: Picador, 2007) 363–72.

as a fellow citizen. We hide them away from public view, and seem to sever the sacred ties that bind them still to our civic and moral conscience. It would be unjust to do that to Arthur Tesler; his ethical slide had been stopped at a precipitous moment, when rehabilitation was still a very real promise and possibility. Balancing the emotional responses of judgment and of mercy is always a challenge in any modern democratic society. As I have noted, Arthur Tesler has been released from federal prison after serving the full term of his sentence. He has now rejoined his family and his community; that is how it is supposed to work. If annual ceremonies of commemoration were ever to be initiated at the Neal Street address, it would be a very fine thing if he were to attend—not to be judged this time, but to be forgiven, by which I mean reintegrated into the moral community, as difficult as that may be for an aggrieved community to imagine or enact.

Given what I learned as a juror about the system of policing we currently have, several obvious strategies to police the state as it polices our streets seem worthy of closer consideration.

First and foremost, serious attention to the mentoring of new police officers who join the narcotics unit seems essential. The almost cavalier and indiscriminate way in which new officers joined up, willy-nilly, with senior officers in that unit seemed overdetermined to produce the results it produced in this case. If these new officers are to be trained in the new skill sets needed for this very dangerous kind of policing, then mentoring in the proper adherence to rules, regulations, and civil rights seems essential. Had Arthur Tesler been assigned different mentors, or been required to work at various times with *everyone* in his unit, then he likely would not have been in the position of coming under my fellow jurors' scrutiny in a court of law.

Second, a number of structural reforms in the actual mechanics of policing seem necessary. The numerical assessment protocols that were utilized for the internal assessment of narcotics investigators has not, to my knowledge, really been addressed. It is difficult to reform a regime whose existence you deny. As I noted in the introduction, quantitative assessment is the norm in any number of important social arenas where it wreaks havoc: in policing, in schooling, and in health care. Since such assessment protocols have everything to do with pay grades, it bears reiterating that our police officers should be better paid. The work they do is dangerous, necessary, often thankless, and utterly civic-minded when it is done well. They should earn enough in doing this work so that they do not need to supplement their incomes with secondary labor. We should view this as the investment in our common good that it so clearly is. Good policing works wonders; bad policing degrades communities.

Much has been written about the unintended consequences of modern technologies, and that too was an unexpected part of this story. Electronic word processors were supposed to save paper. Electronic mail was supposed to save time. Nuclear weapons were supposed to enhance security. And so on. We have created any number of new technologies that enable us to move so fast that we lack the time for more careful and sober reflection. The electronic system whereby police officers can apply for search warrants with a generic application form already on their thumb drives creates the same cut-and-paste mentality that actually invites corner cutting and systematic abuse. If ever there were a situation in which face-to-face discussion should take place,[5] then seeking permission to enter a private citizen's home with weapons drawn is it. We should never forget that little more than two hours separated Fabian Sheats's first lie to these police officers from Ms. Johnston's death in a hail of police gunfire.

Another issue concerns the seemingly never-ending "war on drugs" in which our nation proclaims itself to be perennially engaged. The reform of drug laws that currently invite us to lump all narcotic materials together in one vague fiction called "drugs" seems urgently necessary in the wake of this case. Surely we have the moral maturity, and the common sense, to acknowledge that certain drugs, like alcohol and marijuana, do not pose the same danger to individuals and to the larger society that drugs such as heroin, "crystal meth", and crack cocaine present. The literal mixing up of marijuana and crack cocaine was one of the many striking features of this case.

Moreover, even and especially in the age of Obama, it is important to remain mindful of the historical residue of an older form of racism in our institutions and legal structures. To be sure, we as a society have taken tremendous strides, most of them in a single generation. Dr. King's dream has been realized in part and in places, and the civil rights movement has properly taken its place as a profound moment in the *nation's* history, not just the history of its African-American citizens. Atlanta is the proud home of that significant social memory.

The symbolic importance of this nation's election of its first African-American president, twice, is profound and deep. But it is important to recall David Hollinger's eloquent word of caution to a society that aspires

---

5. On the importance of such face-to-face encounters in democratic conversation, see Jeffrey Stout, *Blessed Are the Organized*, 148–64.

to be post-ethnic: "Racism is real, but races are not."[6] Where narcotics policing and enforcement are concerned, the lingering residue of race-based reasoning is very clear.[7] The war on drugs is waged disproportionately against relatively young black men in this country. Here in Atlanta, our police departments seem fairly well integrated, but the number of African-American men in our prison populations is overwhelmingly out of proportion to the demographics of the city, state, and nation. We do not prosecute this war equally on all fronts, or in all neighborhoods.

Tragically, Neal Street revealed itself to be a literal war zone in this instance. It thus seems both politically advisable and ethically significant to heed the Reverend Anthony Motley's call for some sort of annual commemoration at the Neal Street address. A man deeply informed by the spirituality of the Hebrew Bible, Reverend Motley imagines this as a sort of covenant renewal ceremony, such as the ones enacted by the Israelites upon first entering their land of promise. By calling their past into the present, emphasizing the long journey as the tortuous necessity through which a more just society might be brought into being, the community reminded itself of the covenantal commitments its ancestors had made long ago, and the sacred ties that bound it to an eternal, and as yet unrealized, dream of social justice.[8] We witness the power of such ceremony here in Atlanta each year on the Martin Luther King Jr. holiday, where our commitment to ethno-racial justice is renewed each January at the King Center for Non-violent Social Change, adjacent to the historic Ebenezer Baptist Church. Similar power in the name of a related cause might be generated by such

6. David Hollinger, *Postethnic America: Beyond Multiculturalism*, 2nd ed. (New York: Basic, 2000) 39.

7. I call attention once again to Michelle Alexander's challenging study, *The New Jim Crow: Mass Incarceration in the Age of Colorblindness* (New York: New Press, 2010) esp. 58–94, 173–76.

8. The first such ceremony, presided over by Joshua at Shechem, is described in Joshua 24:1–28; a later form of this ceremony of renewal, organized around the new institution of King Solomon's Temple in Jerusalem, is described in 1 Kings 8:1–66. "Choose this day whom you will serve," Joshua warns, and ticks off the sure punishments that will come to those who abandon the commitments they made that day to their jealous Lord. Sensing the danger, Solomon attempted to refashion the temple as the place where that same Lord would relent, and forgive. While I am less certain about service to such a "jealous" God, I am convinced by the necessary relation these ancient peoples observed between a community that is organized around collective memory and its continued striving toward a more perfect form of social justice.

a November ceremony commemorating Ms. Johnston, Atlanta's unwilling patron saint for vigilance against unjust state-sponsored killing.

Cornel West has been an emphatic and prophetic social critic, calling our collective attention to all such acts of social injustice. The agony of such events is one reason why he speaks so often of the importance of training our youth into the virtues of democratic citizenship. In 2004, he argued eloquently that there were "three dominating, antidemocratic dogmas" that threatened our cultural health and our democratic future: free market fundamentalism; aggressive militarism; and an escalating authoritarianism in the wake of the 9/11 attacks. Though the three are related, it is that third issue that bears greatest relevance to this story. In the never-ending struggle to balance the need for civil liberty and social security, West reminds us that if we as a democratic people do not express our interest in and concern for our civil liberties, then security interests win out by default.[9] The result is inevitably a more antidemocratic form of police state, operating outside of the normal structures of accountability, which is why I have selected the title for this book as I have.

Against this antidemocratic assault on civil liberties, West appealed to three significant moral resources, streams that he imagines still flowing into the mighty river of our common aspirations, our concern for social justice, and the ethical demand of maintaining hope. These streams include, first, civic and Socratic questioning in the spirit of the "wise men" of old Athens; second, the prophetic and even covenantal Jewish commitment to social justice; and third, what West famously calls "the tragicomic commitment to hope." That last idea bears emphasis, since it points to one of West's unique contributions to contemporary social thought, as well as articulating one of the fundamental articles of *his* democratic faith. "The tragicomic hope is expressed in America most profoundly in the wrenchingly honest yet compassionate voices of the black freedom struggle; most poignantly in the painful eloquence of the blues; and most exuberantly in the improvisational virtuosity of jazz."[10]

West is a committed Christian, and as one, he is committed to a rich tradition of "marrying Athens and Jerusalem" in the common cause of modern social justice. Tragicomic hope is, I think, the most fitting name

9. Cornel West, *Democracy Matters: Winning the Fight against Imperialism* (New York: Penguin, 2004), 3–7.

10. Ibid., 16. I note with appreciation the multimedia exhibition "Blues for Smoke," which is currently on display at the Whitney Museum through April 28, 2013. Now back in New York, Cornel West provided a very moving interview for that show.

with which to capture West's distinctive tonality, what we might call his "Good Friday Christianity,"[11] centered on salvific suffering and the cross.

West worked at Princeton for many years with his good friend, Jeffrey Stout, a friend who does not identify in the same way with such Christian conviction. In the introduction, I mentioned Stout's book, *Democracy and Tradition,* as another watershed in my own evolving thinking about democracy; like West's *Democracy Matters*, it was published in 2004. In November 2003, right here in Atlanta, a panel discussion was held in anticipation of the publication of Stout's book. Cornel West offered some superbly appreciative words about the book,[12] then pressed home his own concern with finding the right *tone* in any such social criticism, one that remains mindful of catastrophe, yet finds a way to wrestle toward hope. Here is how Stout responded to the challenge voiced by his friend:

> I want to emphasize that the idea of hope I have in mind when I talk about hope is not a mood but a virtue—the mean between the vices of smug presumption and politically paralyzed despair. So let your mood be as dark as you wish. Let it be as dark as mine. The question of hope is not a question of mood, it is the question of whether we can find it in ourselves . . . to muster the moral fiber to act for justice and to make a difference. If we can't, then our dark mood issues in the vice of despair. You need hope at those moments when you are tempted by that mood . . .[13]

In May 2008, I shared the profound experience of confronting catastrophe with fourteen of my fellow citizens on that jury, and the countless others who worked so diligently and so tirelessly and so seriously to serve the sacred principle that justice must be created, ever anew, if it is ever to be rendered truly. Deliberating in our own halting democratic ways toward an imperfect communion of justice, my fellow citizens appeared to be animated by just such a measured sense of hope. For, as seas surge and storms arise, ever and again, we are called to the sacred service of building

11. I have written about this in an essay titled "Good Friday Christianity," *The Huffington Post* (April 6, 2012). Online: http://www.huffingtonpost.com/louis-a-ruprecht-jr/good-friday-christianity_b_1403279.html.

12. These are echoed by West in *Democracy Matters*, 159–64.

13. Jeffrey Stout, "Pragmatism and Democracy," *The Journal of the American Academy of Religion* 78.2 (2010): 432–33.

Stout offers some persuasive democratic (and secular) translations of the Christian theological virtues—he calls them piety, hope, and love (or charity)—in *Democracy and Tradition*, 9ff.

what Ralph Ellison famously referred to as "a raft of hope." The following memorable passage appeared in his new introduction to the thirty-year anniversary edition of that remarkable novel, *Invisible Man*.

> Here it would seem to me that the interests of art and democracy converge, with the development of conscious, articulate citizens an established goal of this democratic society, and the creation of conscious, articulate characters indispensable to the creation of resonant compositional centers through which an organic consistency can be achieved in the fashioning of fictional forms . . .
>
> So if the ideal of achieving a true political equality eludes us in reality—as it continues to do—there is still available that fictional vision of an ideal democracy in which the actual combines with the ideal and gives us representations of a state of things in which the highly placed and the lowly, the black and the white, the Northerner and the Southerner, the native born and the immigrant combine to tell us of transcendent truths and possibilities such as those discovered when Mark Twain set Huck and Jim afloat on the raft.
>
> Which suggested to me that a novel could be fashioned as a raft of hope, perception and entertainment that might help keep us afloat as we tried to negotiate the snags and whirlpools that mark our nation's vacillating course toward and away from the democratic ideal.[14]

So, a work of art holds up a picture of the democratic ideal that we have not yet achieved in reality. This little book obviously lacks Ellison's artfulness and eloquence, though it shares several of his most notable moral aspirations. It seemed important to me that I try to stay out of the way, editorially speaking, so that the voices of my fellow citizens, "conscious and articulate" in ways that so often surprised and inspired, could be heard more faithfully and more truly. I am not speaking of my fellow jurors alone now, but of all citizens, the criminals included. We the people fashion Ellison's "raft of hope"; we the people, all of us, *have been* that raft.

Such a raft is not an Ark to which we are ordered by divine mandate, two at a time. Democratic citizens are less like Noah, confronting the deluge, and more like Adam after the expulsion, scratching our heads with a gardener's wonder, searching for the words that might name things more properly. The raft Ellison imagines represents a collective democratic

14. *The Collected Essays of Ralph Ellison*, ed. John F. Callahan (New York: Modern Library, 1995) 482–83.

enterprise, fragile to be sure, yet one designed to bring us, if not in a straight line, then haltingly and unerringly closer to our sacred destination: forming a more perfect, and more just, and more forgiving union. The virtue of hope this work requires directs us, not toward some distant Ararat, but to our own nearest neighbors and our most local social commitments, right here, right now. Democracy is not a matter for the hereafter, but for the afterward; our virtue is measured by how we cope with the lethal failures that come inevitably with self-governance, and what we do after we have failed. The three institutions that I have tried to imagine together in this book—schools, hospitals, and courtrooms—are, all three, ultimately structured to be democratic communities commissioned to care. How we care for our tragically departed fellow citizens, and how we tend to the memory of Ms. Kathryn Johnston, will be one measure of the quality of our care.

Bibliography

Alexander, Michelle. *The New Jim Crow: Mass Incarceration in the Age of Colorblindness.* New York: The New Press, 2010.

Alleg, Henri. *The Question.* Translated by John Calder with an original Preface by Jean-Paul Sartre and a new Preface by James D. Le Sueur. Lincoln: University of Nebraska Press, 2006.

Austin, Norman. "Hellenismos." *Arion (Third Series)* 20.1 (2012) 5–36.

Barker, Vanessa. *The Politics of Imprisonment: How the Democratic Process Shapes the Way America Punishes Offenders.* New York: Oxford University Press, 2009.

Brown, Peter. *Through the Eye of a Needle: Wealth, the Fall of Rome, and the Making of Christianity in the West, 350–550 AD.* Princeton, NJ: Princeton University Press, 2012.

Callahan, John F., editor. *The Collected Essays of Ralph Ellison.* New York: The Modern Library, 1995.

Davis, Mike. *City of Quartz: Excavating the Future in Los Angeles.* New York: Vintage, 1990.

———. *Ecology of Fear: Los Angeles and the Imagination of Disaster.* New York: Henry Holt, 1998.

———. "Hell Factories in the Field: A Prison-Industrial Complex." *The Nation* 260.7 (February 20, 1995) 229–33.

Davis, Angela Y. *Angela Davis: An Autobiography.* New York: Random House, 1974.

———. *Are Prisons Obsolete?* New York: Seven Stories, 2003.

———. *The Meaning of Freedom and Other Difficult Dialogues.* San Francisco: City Lights, 2012.

DeNavas-Walt, Carmen, Bernadette D. Proctor, and Jessica C. Smith, et al. "Income, Poverty, and Health Insurance Coverage in the United States: 2010" (US Department of Commerce, September 2011). Online: http://www.census.gov/prod/2011pubs/p60-239.pdf.

Sarah C. Dozier v City of Atlanta (December 21, 2009). Online: http://www.atlantaunfiltered.com/wp-content/uploads/2010/05/kathryn-johnston-undisputed-facts.pdf.

Dunn, Stephen. *Riffs & Reciprocities.* New York: Norton, 1998.

Friedman, Milton, with Rose D. Friedman. *Capitalism and Freedom.* 2nd ed. Chicago: The University of Chicago Press, 1962, 1982.

Harvey, David. *A Brief History of Neoliberalism.* New York: Oxford University Press, 2005.

Haskell, Thomas L. "Capitalism and the Origins of the Humanitarian Sensibility." *The American Historical Review* 90.2 (1985) 339–61 (Part One) and 90.3 (1985) 547–66 (Part Two).

Hollinger, David. *Postethnic America: Beyond Multiculturalism*. 2nd ed. New York: Basic, 1995, 2000.

Klein, Naomi. *The Shock Doctrine: The Rise of Disaster Capitalism*. New York: Picador, 2007.

Laertius, Diogenes. *Lives of the Eminent Philosophers*. 2 vols. Translated by R. D. Hicks. Loeb Classical Library. Cambridge: Harvard University Press, 1972.

Lévêque, Pierre, and Pierre Vidal-Naquet. *Cleisthenes the Athenian: An Essay on the Representation of Space and Time in Greek Political Thought from the End of the Sixth Century BCE to the Death of Plato*. With further essays by Cornelius Castoriadis. Translated by David Ames Curtis. Atlantic Highlands, NJ: Humanities, 1996.

Lewis, Michael. *The Big Short: Inside the Doomsday Machine*. New York: Norton, 2010.

———. *Boomerang: Travels in the New Third World*. New York: Norton, 2011.

Niebuhr, Reinhold. *The Children of Light and the Children of Darkness*. New York: Scribners, 1944.

———. *An Interpretation of Christian Ethics*. New York: Seabury, 1935, 1963.

———. *The Nature and Destiny of Man*. 2 vols. New York: Scribners, 1941, 1943.

———. *The Irony of American History*. New York: Scribners, 1952.

Orwin, Clifford. *The Humanity of Thucydides*. Princeton, NJ: Princeton University Press, 1994.

Patterson, Orlando. *Freedom in the Making of Western Culture*. New York: Basic, 1991.

———. *Slavery and Social Death: A Comparative Study*. Cambridge: Harvard University Press, 1982

Pirro, Robert C. *The Politics of Tragedy and Democratic Citizenship*. New York: Continuum, 2011.

Ramsey, Paul. *Basic Christian Ethics*. Chicago: University of Chicago Press, 1950.

———. *The Just War: Force and Political Responsibility*. New York: Rowman & Littlefield, 1968, 2002.

———. *Nine Modern Moralists*. Englewood Cliffs, NJ: Prentice Hall, 1962.

———. *War and the Christian Conscience: How Shall Modern War Be Conducted Justly?* Durham, NC: Duke University Press, 1961.

Ruprecht, Louis A., Jr. "Good Friday Christianity." *The Huffington Post*, April 2012.

———. *This Tragic Gospel: How John Corrupted the Heart of Christianity*. San Francisco, CA: Jossey-Bass, 2008.

———. *Tragic Posture and Tragic Vision: Against the Modern Failure of Nerve*. New York: Continuum, 1994.

———. *Was Greek Thought Religious? On the Use and Abuse of Hellenism, From Rome to Romanticism* New York: Palgrave Macmillan, 2002.

Schlatter, Richard, editor. *Hobbes's Thucydides*. New Brunswick, NJ: Rutgers University Press, 1975.

Smith, Adam. *An Enquiry into the Nature and Causes of the Wealth of Nations*. Edited by Edwin Cannan. New York: The Modern Library, 1937.

———. *The Theory of Moral Sentiments*. Edited by D. D. Raphael and A. L. Macfie. Indianapolis: Liberty Classics, 1976.

Stern, Philip van Doren, editor. *The Life and Writings of Abraham Lincoln*. New York: The Modern Library, 2000

Stout, Jeffrey. *Blessed are the Organized*. Princeton, NJ: Princeton University Press, 2010.

———. *Democracy and Tradition*. Princeton, NJ: Princeton University Press, 2004.

————. *Ethics After Babel: The Languages of Morals and Their Discontents.* Boston: Beacon, 1988.

————. *The Flight from Authority: Religion, Morality and the Quest for Autonomy.* South Bend, IN: University of Notre Dame Press, 1981.

————, with Stanley Hauerwas, Richard Rorty and Cornel West. "Pragmatism and Democracy." Edited by Jason Springs. *The Journal of the American Academy of Religion* 78.2 (2010) 413–48.

State of Georgia v Arthur Tesler, Fulton County Superior Court, Case #07SC55954.

Tesler v State, 295 Georgia Appeals Reports 569 (2009).

Warner, Rex, editor and translator. *The Peloponnesian War.* New York: Penguin, 1954.

Weil, Simone. "The Iliad, or the Poem of Force." Reprinted in *On Violence: A Reader,* edited by Bruce B. Lawrence and Aisha Karim. Durham, NC: Duke University Press, 2002, 377–90.

West, Cornel. *The American Evasion of Philosophy: A Genealogy of Pragmatism.* Minneapolis: University of Minnesota Press, 1989.

————. *The Cornel West Reader.* New York: Basic Civitas, 1999.

————. *Democracy Matters: Winning the Fight Against Imperialism.* New York: Penguin, 2004.

————. *Prophecy Deliverance! An Afro-American Revolutionary Christianity.* Louisville: Westminster John Knox, 1982, 2002.

————. *Race Matters.* New York: Vintage, 2001.